Ansible DevOps Cookbook

End-to-end automation solutions including setup, playbooks, cloud services, CI/CD integration, and ansible tower management

Thorne Montgomery

Published by: GitforGits

Publisher: Sonal Dhandre

www.gitforgits.com

support@gitforgits.com

Printed in India

First Printing: July 2024

ISBN: 978-81-19177-73-8

Cover Design by: Kitten Publishing

Prologue

When I first discovered Ansible, it felt like finding a hidden gem in the vast world of DevOps tools. I remember how exciting it was to write my first playbook and be amazed as tasks that used to take hours to do by hand were done perfectly in seconds. That moment made me want to automate things and be more efficient, which is why I wrote the "Ansible DevOps Cookbook."

My association with Ansible began in Seattle on a rainy night. My job at the time was as a DevOps engineer for a medium-sized tech company. We were in the middle of a big deployment. Our old ways of doing things were slow and prone to mistakes, which caused delays and frustration. Ansible came up for me while I was looking for answers. I chose to give it a try because it seemed like it would be easy to use and powerful. I learned Ansible, played around with playbooks, and automated tasks that used to give me a headache over the next few weeks. The results were truly amazing. Ansible speeding up and improved the reliability of our deployments, giving our team more time to work on new ideas instead of doing the same things over and over again. When word got out about how well we did, other teams in the company asked me to help them add Ansible to their workflows. As I learned more about Ansible, I realized that the official documentation and tutorials were helpful, but I needed a guide that was more hands-on and useful. Something that would not only teach the basics but also give DevOps professionals real-world answers to problems they often face. This thought led to the creation of the "Ansible DevOps Cookbook."

With this book, I wanted to make a reliable tool that would help anyone get the most out of Ansible. I started making notes, writing down recipes, and asking coworkers and peers for feedback. There were a lot of hours spent trying out, testing, and improving every recipe in this book. One of the most memorable parts of writing this book was a late-night meeting with my team to come up with ideas. We were trying to figure out a very tricky problem with dynamic inventories in a setting with more than one cloud. After many failed attempts and many cups of coffee, inspiration finally struck. We came up with a solution that worked and made the whole process easier. This recipe, like many others in this book, shows how important it is to work together and keep going.

There are more than 100 recipes that are meant to help you solve problems in the real world. With this book, you can learn everything from how to set up your Ansible environment to advanced playbook techniques, cloud integration, CI/CD pipelines, and fixing problems. Each recipe is designed to give you useful solutions, which makes it easy to use Ansible and get the most out of it. As you read this book, keep in mind that every great story about automation starts with a single guide. I hope this book becomes your go-to guide and motivates you to discover new things about DevOps automation. We can make the impossible seem possible and difficult tasks run like clockwork if we work together.

Content

Preface

A collection of over seventy-five solution-focused recipes, "Ansible DevOps Cookbook" will show you how to use Ansible to fix problems, simplify operations, and boost the efficiency of your DevOps practices. Clear, step-by-step directions are provided for every recipe in this cookbook, covering everything from basic setup to advanced techniques.

You should start by creating an efficient inventory system, configuring control and managed nodes, and setting up your Ansible environment. You can implement effective solutions because the recipes address specific challenges. Get a handle on more complex playbook techniques, such as working with variables, facts, conditionals, loops, and more. You will be skillful to organize playbooks and create reusable automation with Ansible roles. You can increase your automation capabilities by accessing community-driven content through Ansible Galaxy, which is explained in the book.

When it comes to cloud integration, the book goes into great detail on how to automate deployments on AWS, Azure, and GCP. These recipes show how to use Ansible modules for managing and provisioning cloud infrastructure, so you can manage resources efficiently and ensure high availability and performance. Ansible, Jenkins, and GitLab are among the many of the tools covered in this book, which teaches you to automate the build, test, and deployment pipeline as part of continuous integration and continuous delivery.

From playbook errors to inventory management issues, this cookbook has solutions to fix it all. Ansible Tower and AWX are implemented in the last chapters to automate enterprise-grade tasks, including job scheduling, monitoring, and role-based access control. This book's practical, real-world solutions will help you improve your DevOps practices and maximize the effectiveness of Ansible in your automation processes.

In this book you will learn how to:

- Gain the expertise and abilities needed to establish Ansible environments for efficient automation and management of DevOps processes.
- Discover sophisticated playbook strategies for optimizing task automation through the utilization of variables and handlers.
- Streamline cloud deployments on AWS, Azure, and GCP to ensure optimal availability and performance.
- Integrate Ansible with CI/CD tools such as Jenkins and GitLab to enable continuous delivery.
- Resolve playbook errors and address inventory management issues using effective solutions.

- Employ Ansible roles and Galaxy to implement scalable and reusable automation content.
- Deploy high-level automation using Ansible Tower and AWX, which includes robust role-based access control.
- Efficiently manage workflow by scheduling and monitoring Ansible jobs.
- Efficiently oversee both dynamic and static inventories, guaranteeing accurate allocation of resources.

GitforGits

Prerequisites

Whether you are an IT administrator, networking professional, cloud engineer or a devops user, this book is meant for you to learn troubleshooting every possible issue, streamline processes, and maximize the performance of your IT infrsastructure and DevOps processes.

Codes Usage

Are you in need of some helpful code examples to assist you in your programming and documentation? Look no further! Our book offers a wealth of supplemental material, including code examples and exercises.

Not only is this book here to aid you in getting your job done, but you have our permission to use the example code in your programs and documentation. However, please note that if you are reproducing a significant portion of the code, we do require you to contact us for permission.

But don't worry, using several chunks of code from this book in your program or answering a question by citing our book and quoting example code does not require permission. But if you do choose to give credit, an attribution typically includes the title, author, publisher, and ISBN. For example, "Ansible DevOps Cookbook by Thorne Montgomery".

If you are unsure whether your intended use of the code examples falls under fair use or the permissions outlined above, please do not hesitate to reach out to us at support@gitforgits.com.

We are happy to assist and clarify any concerns.

Acknowledgement

I owe a tremendous debt of gratitude to GitforGits, for their unflagging enthusiasm and wise counsel throughout the entire process of writing this book. Their knowledge and careful editing helped make sure the piece was useful for people of all reading levels and comprehension skills. In addition, I'd like to thank everyone involved in the publishing process for their efforts in making this book a reality. Their efforts, from copyediting to advertising, made the project what it is today.

Finally, I'd like to express my gratitude to everyone who has shown me unconditional love and encouragement throughout my life. Their support was crucial to the completion of this book. I appreciate your help with this endeavour and your continued interest in my career.

CHAPTER 1: UP AND RUNNING WITH ANSIBLE ENVIRONMENT

Introduction

The purpose of this chapter is to teach you how to set up and configure your Ansible environment, which will provide you with a solid foundation for managing and automating your infrastructure. Starting with Ansible on Linux, you will be taken through the steps required to get Ansible up and running on your system. This includes configuring Ansible control nodes, which serve as the primary management points for your automation tasks, allowing you to efficiently manage multiple hosts.

You will also create an Ansible project specifically for the GitforGits web application, allowing you to apply the concepts you have learned to a real-world example. The setup of SSH key-based authentication will be learned, which is a crucial step in securing and optimizing your connections to remote hosts. You'll also learn how to properly organize your Ansible directory structure, which is critical for keeping a clean and manageable code base.

Another important topic is managing the Ansible configuration files. This will make sure that your Ansible environment is customized to your specific requirements and workflows. The chapter will also walk you through the process of creating a local virtual development environment, which will serve as a sandbox for testing and refining automation scripts without affecting your production systems. Finally, you will connect to remote hosts, allowing you to easily manage and automate tasks across multiple machines.

After reading this chapter, you will know everything there is to know about configuring an Ansible environment on Linux. You will be able to manage your infrastructure more effectively with these basic skills, which will also prepare you for the more advanced automation tasks that will be covered in later chapters.

Recipe #1: Installing Ansible on Linux

To begin using Ansible, you first need to install it on your Linux system. This recipe will instruct you on the installation process, ensuring that you have Ansible ready to manage and automate your infrastructure.

Update Package Manager

Before installing any new software, it's a good practice to update your package manager to ensure you have the latest package lists. Open your terminal and run:

```
sudo apt update
```

Install Ansible

Once your package manager is updated, you can proceed with the Ansible installation. For Debian-based systems like Ubuntu, use the following command:

```
sudo apt install ansible -y
```

For Red Hat-based systems like CentOS, first enable the EPEL repository:

```
sudo yum install epel-release -y
```

Then install Ansible:

```
sudo yum install ansible -y
```

Verify Installation

After the installation is complete, verify that Ansible is installed correctly by checking its version:

```
ansible --version
```

You should see the Ansible version and other relevant information, indicating that Ansible is installed and ready to use.

By following these steps, you have successfully installed Ansible on your Linux system. This installation is the first step in setting up your environment, allowing you to start creating and running playbooks for automating tasks across your infrastructure.

Recipe #2: Configuring Ansible Control Nodes

A control node is a machine where you install Ansible, and from which you manage and automate tasks across multiple hosts. The control node is essential in Ansible architecture, serving as the central point for running Ansible commands and managing configurations. This recipe will teach you in setting up and configuring your control node to ensure smooth operations.

Verify SSH Access

Ensure that you can connect to the target machines via SSH. Generate an SSH key if you haven't already:

```
ssh-keygen
```

Copy the SSH key to the target machines:

```
ssh-copy-id user@target_machine
```

Edit Ansible Hosts File

Ansible uses an inventory file to keep track of the machines it manages. Edit the default inventory file located at **/etc/ansible/hosts**:

```
sudo nano /etc/ansible/hosts
```

Add your target machines, organizing them into groups if needed:

```
[webservers]

web1.gitforgits.com

web2.gitforgits.com



[databases]

db1.gitforgits.com

db2.gitforgits.com
```

Test Connectivity

Test the connectivity to your target machines using the Ansible ping module:

```
ansible all -m ping
```

You should see a success message for each target machine, indicating that the control node can connect to them.

Configure ansible.cfg

Customize Ansible's behavior by editing the **ansible.cfg** file. You can create this configuration file in your project directory:

```
nano ansible.cfg
```

Add basic configurations:

```
[defaults]

inventory = /etc/ansible/hosts

remote_user = your_user

host_key_checking = False
```

With this, you have successfully configured your Ansible control node. This configuration allows you to manage and automate tasks across multiple machines, laying the groundwork for more advanced Ansible operations.

Recipe #3: Initializing Ansible Project (Ex. GitforGits Project)

With the control node configured, the next step is to initialize your Ansible project for the GitforGits web application. This recipe will teach you in setting up the project structure and preparing it for managing and automating tasks.

Create Project Directory

Start by creating a directory for your Ansible project. This will be the root directory where all your playbooks, inventory files, and configuration files are stored:

```
mkdir ~/GitforGits

cd ~/GitforGits
```

Setup Directory Structure

Organize your project directory by creating subdirectories for playbooks, inventory, roles, and configuration files. This structure helps maintain a clean and manageable codebase:

```
mkdir playbooks inventory roles
```

Create Inventory File

In the **inventory** directory, create a file named **hosts** to list the target machines you will manage. Refer to the configuration steps in Recipe #2 if needed:

```
nano inventory/hosts
```

Add your target machines:

```
[webservers]

web1.gitforgits.com

web2.gitforgits.com


[databases]

db1.gitforgits.com

db2.gitforgits.com
```

Create a Playbook

In the **playbooks** directory, create a file named **site.yml** as your main playbook. This playbook will define tasks for managing the GitforGits application:

```
nano playbooks/site.yml
```

Add a basic playbook structure:

```
---

- hosts: all

  tasks:

    - name: Ensure Nginx is installed
```

```
    apt:
      name: nginx
      state: present
    become: yes
```

Ensure your project is using the correct Ansible configuration by creating an **ansible.cfg** file in the project root directory. Refer to the configuration steps in Recipe #2 if needed:

```
nano ansible.cfg
```

Add basic configurations:

```
[defaults]
inventory = inventory/hosts
remote_user = your_user
host_key_checking = False
```

This above outlined setup will allow you to organize and manage your playbooks and inventory efficiently, providing a solid foundation for automating tasks related to GitforGits.

Recipe #4: Setting up SSH Key-based Authentication

Authentication is quite a needy mechanism for managing remote machines securely, and there are several types of authentication methods available, including password-based, token-based, and key-based authentication. Password-based authentication requires you to enter a password each time you connect to a remote machine. While simple, it poses security risks such as susceptibility to brute-force attacks. Token-based authentication uses time-sensitive tokens and is commonly used in multi-factor authentication scenarios.

Key-based authentication, on the other hand, is considered more secure and efficient. It uses a pair of cryptographic keys: a public key stored on the remote machine and a private key stored securely on your control node. This method eliminates the need for password entry during connections, reduces the risk of brute-force attacks, and allows for automated, secure connections.

This recipe sets up SSH key-based authentication to have secure and automated connections between your control node and remote hosts.

Generate SSH Key Pair

First, generate an SSH key pair on your control node if you don't already have one.

Open a terminal and run:

```
ssh-keygen
```

Follow the prompts to save the key pair in the default location (**~/.ssh/id_rsa**). You can choose to add a passphrase for additional security.

Copy Public Key to Remote Hosts

Next, copy the public key to each remote host. This step authorizes your control node to connect to the remote host using the private key:

```
ssh-copy-id user@remote_host
```

Replace **user** and **remote_host** with the appropriate username and hostname or IP address of the remote machine. Repeat this step for each remote host.

Verify SSH Key-based Authentication

Test the connection to each remote host to ensure that key-based authentication is set up correctly:

```
ssh user@remote_host
```

If the setup is correct, you should be able to connect without being prompted for a password.

Then, update your **ansible.cfg** file to ensure Ansible uses the correct SSH key for connections:

```
nano ansible.cfg
```

Add or update the following settings:

```
[defaults]

inventory = inventory/hosts

remote_user = your_user

private_key_file = ~/.ssh/id_rsa

host_key_checking = False
```

With this, you have successfully set up SSH key-based authentication for your Ansible control node. Which ultimately improves the efficiency of your Ansible operations.

Recipe #5: Organizing Ansible Directory Structure

A well-organized directory structure is crucial for maintaining a clean and manageable Ansible project. This recipe will demonstrate in setting up a structured directory layout for the GitforGits project. Referring back to Recipe #3, where you initialized the GitforGits project, we will build on that foundation to organize your files and directories effectively.

In this recipe, we create a logical and organized directory structure for your Ansible project, ensuring that playbooks, inventories, roles, and configuration files are easy to manage and navigate.

Review Existing Directory Structure

In Recipe #3, you created the basic project directories. Let's revisit and expand on that structure:

```
mkdir ~/GitforGits

cd ~/GitforGits

mkdir playbooks inventory roles group_vars host_vars
```

Create Group and Host Variables Directories

Group and host variables allow you to define specific configurations for groups of hosts or individual hosts. Create these directories within your project:

```
mkdir group_vars host_vars
```

Place your playbooks in the **playbooks** directory. You can create subdirectories within **playbooks** for better organization, especially if you have multiple playbooks:

```
mkdir playbooks/setup playbooks/deploy
playbooks/maintenance
```

Define Roles

Roles help you organize tasks, handlers, variables, files, templates, and modules. Create a basic role structure within the **roles** directory:

```
mkdir -p
roles/common/{tasks,handlers,templates,files,vars,default
s,meta}
```

Ensure your **ansible.cfg** file points to the correct inventory and roles paths. Refer to Recipe #2 for initial configuration details. Update **ansible.cfg** as follows:

```
[defaults]

inventory = inventory/hosts

remote_user = your_user

roles_path = roles

host_key_checking = False
```

Sample File Placement

Following is a brief example of where to place files:

- Inventory file: **`inventory/hosts`**
- Group variables: **`group_vars/webservers.yml`**
- Host variables: **`host_vars/web1.gitforgits.com.yml`**
- Main playbook: **`playbooks/site.yml`**
- Role tasks: **`roles/common/tasks/main.yml`**

This above structure ensures that your Ansible configurations are modular, scalable, and easy to manage for efficient development and automation workflows.

Recipe #6: Managing Ansible Configuration Files

The Ansible configuration file, typically named **ansible.cfg** defines how Ansible behaves during execution. This file allows you to customize various settings such as inventory paths, remote user details, and plugin configurations. The **ansible.cfg** file is a plain text file that consists of various sections, each containing configuration options. The primary sections include **[defaults]**, **[privilege_escalation]**, **[ssh_connection]**, and others. Each section allows you to define specific parameters that control Ansible's behavior, such as default inventory file location, remote user settings, and SSH connection options.

In this recipe, we will manage and customize the Ansible configuration file to optimize your Ansible environment for the GitforGits project.

Locate Configuration File

The **ansible.cfg** file can be located in several places, including:

- In your project directory
- In your home directory (**`~/.ansible.cfg`**)
- In **`/etc/ansible/ansible.cfg`**

For project-specific configurations, create the **ansible.cfg** file in your GitforGits project directory:

```
cd ~/GitforGits

nano ansible.cfg
```

Basic Configuration

Start by configuring the basic settings in the **[defaults]** section. This includes setting the inventory file path and the default remote user:

```
[defaults]

inventory = inventory/hosts
```

```
remote_user = your_user

roles_path = roles

host_key_checking = False
```

Privilege Escalation Settings

If your playbooks require running tasks with elevated privileges, configure the **[privilege_escalation]** section:

```
[privilege_escalation]

become = True

become_method = sudo

become_user = root

become_ask_pass = False
```

SSH Connection Settings

Customize SSH connection options in the **[ssh_connection]** section to optimize the performance and security of SSH connections:

```
[ssh_connection]

ssh_args = -o ControlMaster=auto -o ControlPersist=60s

pipelining = True
```

Testing and Validation

After updating the **ansible.cfg** file, test your configuration by running a simple Ansible command to ensure it's correctly applied:

```
ansible all -m ping
```

This command should execute without errors, confirming that your configuration is valid and operational.

Recipe #7: Setting up a Local Virtual Development Environment

To test and develop Ansible playbooks without affecting your production systems, setting up a local virtual development environment is crucial. In this recipe, you will use Vagrant. Vagrant is an open-source tool that provides easy-to-configure, reproducible, and portable work environments. It uses simple configuration files to set up virtual machines (VMs) and integrates well with various providers like VirtualBox, VMware, and Docker. Vagrant makes it easy to manage VMs, ensuring consistent environments for development and testing.

In this recipe, we will set up a local virtual development environment using Vagrant, allowing you to develop and test Ansible playbooks for the GitforGits project.

Install Vagrant

First, install Vagrant on your Linux system. Download the appropriate package from the Vagrant website and install it. You can use:

```
sudo apt update

sudo apt install -y vagrant
```

Install VirtualBox

Vagrant works with various providers, but VirtualBox is commonly used due to its compatibility and ease of use. Install VirtualBox from the VirtualBox website or use your package manager:

```
sudo apt install -y virtualbox
```

Initialize Vagrant Project

Create a directory for your Vagrant project and initialize it. This will create a **Vagrantfile**, which defines the configuration of your virtual environment:

```
mkdir ~/GitforGitsVagrant

cd ~/GitforGitsVagrant
```

```
vagrant init
```

Configure Vagrantfile

Edit the **Vagrantfile** to define the VM settings. Open the **Vagrantfile** in a text editor:

```
nano Vagrantfile
```

Modify the file to configure a basic VM. Given below is an example configuration:

```
Vagrant.configure("2") do |config|

  config.vm.box = "ubuntu/bionic64"

  config.vm.network "private_network", type: "dhcp"

  config.vm.provider "virtualbox" do |vb|

    vb.memory = "1024"

    vb.cpus = 2

  end

end
```

Start and Provision the VM

Start the VM using Vagrant. This command will create and configure the VM as defined in the **Vagrantfile**:

```
vagrant up
```

Once the VM is up and running, you can SSH into it:

```
vagrant ssh
```

Integrate with Ansible

You can now use this VM as a target for your Ansible playbooks. Update your Ansible inventory file to include the Vagrant VM. Find the IP address of the VM using **vagrant ssh-config** or by logging into the VM and using **ifconfig**.

Add the VM to your **inventory/hosts** file:

```
[development]

192.168.56.101 ansible_ssh_user=vagrant
ansible_ssh_private_key_file=~/.vagrant.d/insecure_privat
e_key
```

With this, you have successfully set up a local virtual development environment using Vagrant.

Recipe #8: Connecting to Remote Hosts

Connecting to remote hosts is a fundamental aspect of using Ansible for automation and management tasks. This recipe will practically walkthrough the process of setting up and verifying connections to your remote hosts from the Ansible control node. The objective of this recipe is to establish and verify secure connections to remote hosts, enabling Ansible to manage and automate tasks across multiple machines.

Ensure SSH Key-based Authentication

Refer back to Recipe #4, where you set up SSH key-based authentication. Ensure that the public key is copied to all remote hosts you wish to manage. This step is critical for seamless, passwordless connections.

Update Inventory File

Add your remote hosts to the Ansible inventory file. Open the inventory file you created in Recipe #3 and add the IP addresses or hostnames of your remote machines:

```
[webservers]

web1.gitforgits.com

web2.gitforgits.com
```

```
[databases]

db1.gitforgits.com

db2.gitforgits.com
```

Test SSH Connectivity

Before using Ansible to manage your hosts, manually test SSH connectivity to each remote host:

```
ssh user@web1.gitforgits.com
```

Ensure that you can connect without being prompted for a password.

Verify Ansible Connectivity

Use Ansible's ping module to verify connectivity to all hosts in your inventory. This command sends a ping to each host and returns the result:

```
ansible all -m ping
```

You should see success messages for all the hosts listed in your inventory, confirming that Ansible can connect to them.

Troubleshoot Connection Issues

If you encounter any connection issues, check the following:

- Ensure the SSH key is correctly copied to the remote host.
- Verify that the remote user has the necessary permissions.
- Confirm the remote host's IP address or hostname is correct.
- Check for any firewall rules or network issues that might be blocking the connection.

Configure SSH Options

Update the **ansible.cfg** file to include any necessary SSH options. Open the configuration file and add or update the **[ssh_connection]** section:

```
[ssh_connection]

ssh_args = -o ControlMaster=auto -o ControlPersist=60s
```

```
pipelining = True
```

Test Playbook Execution

Run a simple playbook to ensure that Ansible can execute tasks on your remote hosts. Create a playbook **test.yml** in the **playbooks** directory:

```
---

- hosts: all

  tasks:

    - name: Test connectivity

      command: echo "Hello from Ansible"
```

Execute the playbook:

```
ansible-playbook playbooks/test.yml
```

This setup allows Ansible to manage and automate tasks across your infrastructure, ensuring efficient and secure operations. This completes the foundational chapter on getting up and running with the Ansible environment, preparing you for more advanced tasks in subsequent chapters.

Summary

Chapter 1 taught you how to set up and configure the Ansible environment, beginning with the installation of Ansible on Linux systems. In this chapter, you learned how to set up Ansible control nodes and how they work as hubs for managing automation jobs. You started the Ansible project for the GitforGits web application, which provides a foundation for managing configurations and playbooks. To improve the safety and efficiency of connections to remote hosts, SSH key-based authentication was implemented. You organized the Ansible directory structure to ensure a clean and manageable project layout, including directories for playbooks, inventory, roles, group variables, and host variables.

Ansible configuration file management was covered, with options for customizing inventory paths, remote user details, privilege escalation, and SSH connection settings. In order to build and test Ansible playbooks in a controlled environment, away from live production systems, you can use Vagrant to set up a local virtual development environment. This included installing Vagrant and VirtualBox, setting up a Vagrant project, configuring the Vagrantfile, and integrating the Vagrant virtual machines with Ansible.

Finally, you connected to remote hosts to test SSH connectivity and Ansible's ability to manage and automate tasks on multiple machines. This included testing SSH key-based connections, updating the Ansible inventory file, and utilizing the Ansible ping module to ensure successful communication with remote hosts. Additionally, we covered how to configure SSH options in the Ansible configuration file, test the execution of the playbook to ensure a successful setup, and troubleshoot common connection issues.

With the knowledge you gained in this chapter, you should be able to install, configure, initialize projects, establish secure connections, organize directories, and test Ansible on Linux. This will set you up well for more complex automation tasks.

Knowledge Exercise

Question 1: What is the primary role of an Ansible control node?

A) To act as a backup server
B) To run and manage Ansible commands and configurations
C) To store inventory files
D) To host web applications

Answer:
B) To run and manage Ansible commands and configurations

The control node is the central point where Ansible commands are executed and managed. It controls the automation processes for remote hosts.

Question 2: Which command is used to install Ansible on a Debian-based Linux system?

A) **`sudo yum install ansible -y`**
B) **`sudo apt install ansible -y`**
C) **`sudo dnf install ansible -y`**
D) **`sudo install ansible -y`**

Answer:
B) **`sudo apt install ansible -y`**

For Debian-based systems like Ubuntu, the **`apt`** package manager is used to install Ansible.

Question 3: How can you verify that Ansible is correctly installed on your system?
A) **`ansible --check`**
B) **`ansible --validate`**
C) **`ansible --version`**
D) **`ansible --test`**

Answer:
C) **`ansible --version`**

Running **`ansible --version`** provides information about the installed Ansible version and confirms its presence on the system.

Question 4: Which file is edited to add remote hosts for Ansible management?
A) **`inventory.txt`**
B) **`hosts.cfg`**
C) **`ansible_hosts`**
D) **`/etc/ansible/hosts`**

Answer:
D) **`/etc/ansible/hosts`**

The **`/etc/ansible/hosts`** file is the default inventory file where remote hosts are listed for Ansible to manage.

Question 5: What is the purpose of SSH key-based authentication in Ansible?
A) To use passwords for secure connections
B) To eliminate the need for passwords during SSH connections
C) To connect using a graphical interface
D) To improve network speed

Answer:
B) To eliminate the need for passwords during SSH connections

SSH key-based authentication enhances security and efficiency by allowing passwordless SSH connections using cryptographic keys.

Question 6: Which command copies the public SSH key to a remote host?
A) **`ssh-copy-id user@remote_host`**
B) **`ssh-keygen user@remote_host`**
C) **`ssh-add user@remote_host`**
D) **`scp-key user@remote_host`**

Answer:
A) **ssh-copy-id user@remote_host**

The **ssh-copy-id** command is used to copy the public SSH key to a remote host, enabling key-based authentication.

Question 7: What is the significance of the **ansible.cfg** file in an Ansible project?
A) It stores playbooks
B) It defines how Ansible behaves during execution
C) It contains inventory details
D) It holds the source code of Ansible modules

Answer:
B) It defines how Ansible behaves during execution

The **ansible.cfg** file allows customization of Ansible's behavior, such as setting inventory paths and configuring SSH options.

Question 8: Which command is used to initialize a Vagrant project for setting up a local virtual environment?
A) **vagrant start**
B) **vagrant init**
C) **vagrant create**
D) **vagrant setup**

Answer:
B) **vagrant init**

The **vagrant init** command initializes a Vagrant project and creates a **Vagrantfile** to define the VM configuration.

Question 9: What information is typically found in the **[defaults]** section of the **ansible.cfg** file?
A) SSH key details
B) Remote user and inventory file path
C) Database credentials
D) Network configurations

Answer:
B) Remote user and inventory file path

The **[defaults]** section of the **ansible.cfg** file contains settings such as the default inventory file path and the remote user.

Question 10: Which command can be used to test connectivity to all hosts listed in the Ansible inventory?
A) **`ansible all -m ping`**
B) **`ansible all -m test`**
C) **`ansible all -m connect`**
D) **`ansible all -m ssh`**

Answer:
A) **`ansible all -m ping`**

The **`ansible all -m ping`** command sends a ping to all hosts in the inventory to verify connectivity.

Question 11: Why is it important to organize the Ansible directory structure?
A) To increase network speed
B) To keep the project clean and manageable
C) To reduce the size of inventory files
D) To make Ansible run faster

Answer:
B) To keep the project clean and manageable

A well-organized directory structure helps maintain clarity and manageability, especially in larger projects.

Question 12: Which directory in an Ansible project is typically used to store playbooks?
A) **`roles`**
B) **`playbooks`**
C) **`inventory`**
D) **`vars`**

Answer:
B) **`playbooks`**

The **`playbooks`** directory is used to store playbook files, which contain the automation tasks to be executed by Ansible.

Question 13: What is the role of the **`group_vars`** and **`host_vars`** directories in an Ansible project?
A) To store playbooks

B) To define variables for groups and hosts
C) To hold the **ansible.cfg** file
D) To list remote hosts

Answer:
B) To define variables for groups and hosts

The **group_vars** and **host_vars** directories are used to define variables specific to groups of hosts or individual hosts.

Question 14: Which Vagrant command is used to start the virtual machine defined in the **Vagrantfile**?
A) **vagrant boot**
B) **vagrant up**
C) **vagrant start**
D) **vagrant init**

Answer:
B) **vagrant up**

The **vagrant up** command starts the virtual machine as defined in the **Vagrantfile**.

Question 15: How do you SSH into a Vagrant-managed virtual machine?
A) **vagrant connect**
B) **vagrant ssh**
C) **vagrant login**
D) **vagrant access**

Answer:
B) **vagrant ssh**

The **vagrant ssh** command is used to SSH into a Vagrant-managed virtual machine.

Question 16: What does the **hosts** directive in an Ansible playbook specify?
A) The inventory file location
B) The remote user
C) The target machines for the playbook
D) The SSH key file

Answer:
C) The target machines for the playbook

The **hosts** directive in a playbook specifies which machines the playbook should run on.

Question 17: Why might you configure **ControlMaster** and **ControlPersist** options in the **[ssh_connection]** section of **ansible.cfg**?
A) To increase disk space
B) To optimize SSH connections
C) To enable graphical interfaces
D) To store passwords

Answer:
B) To optimize SSH connections

ControlMaster and **ControlPersist** options optimize SSH connections by allowing multiple sessions to share a single connection.

Question 18: What command is used to create a new SSH key pair?
A) **ssh-copy-id**
B) **ssh-keygen**
C) **ssh-add**
D) **ssh-config**

Answer:
B) **ssh-keygen**

The **ssh-keygen** command generates a new SSH key pair.

Question 19: In which section of the **ansible.cfg** file do you set the method for privilege escalation?
A) **[ssh_connection]**
B) **[privilege_escalation]**
C) **[defaults]**
D) **[inventory]**

Answer:
B) **[privilege_escalation]**

The **[privilege_escalation]** section is used to configure how Ansible should handle privilege escalation, such as using **sudo**.

Question 20: How do you add a new remote host to the Ansible inventory file?
A) By editing the **ansible.cfg** file
B) By running **ansible-inventory --add**

C) By adding the host entry to the **`/etc/ansible/hosts`** file
D) By creating a new playbook

Answer:
C) By adding the host entry to the **`/etc/ansible/hosts`** file

To add a new remote host, you edit the **`/etc/ansible/hosts`** file and include the host details.

Chapter 2: Writing and Running Playbooks

Introduction

In the preceding chapter, you acquired the knowledge necessary to establish and configure your Ansible environment. Ansible was installed, control nodes were configured, the GitforGits project was initialized, SSH key-based authentication was set up, directory structure was organized, configuration files were managed, a local virtual environment was created with Vagrant, and remote hosts were connected to. Now that you have finished the basic steps, you can move on to the meat and potatoes of Ansible automation: writing and running playbooks.

You will learn how to make and organize playbooks in this chapter. The initial step is to develop your initial playbook, which serves as a base for all automation tasks. If you want to write automation scripts that are more dynamic and flexible, you need to learn how to use variables and facts within playbooks. In this chapter, you will find out how to use conditionals so that playbooks can evaluate situations using predefined criteria and how to loop over tasks so that repetitive operations can be executed more efficiently.

It is essential to debug playbook errors in order to ensure the smooth operation of your automation scripts and to troubleshoot concerns. You will explore the methods for recognizing and resolving common problems that may occur. When you use handlers for task notifications, you can efficiently and responsively automate tasks that need to be triggered by changes. By reusing tasks and dividing intricate playbooks into manageable components, the organization of playbooks with includes and imports will ensure that your codebase remains clean and maintainable. At last, you'll find out how to use Ansible's power to automate and manage tasks on a large scale by running playbooks across multiple machines.

After finishing this chapter, you will know everything there is to know about Ansible playbooks and how to write and run them.

Recipe #1: Creating First Playbook

Creating first playbook is a significant step in utilizing Ansible for automation. A playbook is a YAML file that defines a set of tasks to be executed on specified hosts. This recipe will practically walkthrough the process of writing and running a simple playbook. In this recipe, we will create a basic Ansible playbook that performs a simple task on a remote host, laying the foundation for more complex automation tasks.

Understand Playbook Structure

A playbook consists of one or more plays. Each play targets a group of hosts and defines tasks to be executed. Following is a basic structure:

```
---
```

```
- name: Ensure Nginx is installed
  hosts: webservers
  become: yes
  tasks:
    - name: Install Nginx
      apt:
        name: nginx
        state: present
```

Create a new playbook file in your **playbooks** directory:

```
nano ~/GitforGits/playbooks/first_playbook.yml
```

Define Play and Tasks

Copy the given below script into your playbook file. This playbook ensures that Nginx is installed on all hosts in the **webservers** group:

```
---
- name: Ensure Nginx is installed
  hosts: webservers
  become: yes
  tasks:
    - name: Install Nginx
      apt:
        name: nginx
```

```
        state: present
```

Save the changes and close the text editor.

Run the Playbook

Execute the playbook using the **ansible-playbook** command:

```
ansible-playbook
~/GitforGits/playbooks/first_playbook.yml
```

This command will run the playbook on all hosts in the **webservers** group, installing Nginx if it is not already present.

Verify the Results

After running the playbook, verify that Nginx is installed on the target hosts by accessing them and checking the service status:

```
ssh user@web1.gitforgits.com

sudo systemctl status nginx
```

This playbook serves as a foundation for building more complex automation tasks, allowing you to efficiently manage and configure your infrastructure.

Recipe #2: Using Variables and Facts in Playbooks

Variables and facts are fundamental elements in Ansible playbooks that allow for dynamic and flexible automation. Variables store values that can be reused throughout your playbooks, while facts are automatically gathered information about the remote hosts, such as IP addresses, operating system details, and hardware specifications.

Advanced Aspects of Variables and Facts

Variables can be defined in multiple ways, including directly in playbooks, in inventory files, or in separate variable files. They can also be passed as extra variables during playbook execution. Ansible facts are gathered by the **setup** module, which collects details about the remote hosts and makes them accessible within your playbooks.

The learnings behind this recipe is to demonstrate the use of variables and facts in Ansible playbooks to create more dynamic and adaptable automation scripts.

Define Variables in Playbooks

Variables can be defined directly within a playbook under the **vars** section:

```
nano ~/GitforGits/playbooks/variables_playbook.yml
```

Put the following snippet:

```
---
- name: Using Variables and Facts
  hosts: webservers
  become: yes
  vars:
    package_name: nginx
    service_name: nginx
  tasks:
    - name: Install a package
      apt:
        name: "{{ package_name }}"
        state: present

    - name: Ensure the service is running
      service:
```

```
        name: "{{ service_name }}"
        state: started
```

Use Facts in Playbooks

Facts are automatically gathered and can be accessed using the **ansible_facts** dictionary. Modify the playbook to use a fact:

```
---
- name: Using Variables and Facts
  hosts: webservers
  become: yes
  vars:
    package_name: nginx
    service_name: nginx
  tasks:
    - name: Install a package
      apt:
        name: "{{ package_name }}"
        state: present

    - name: Ensure the service is running
      service:
        name: "{{ service_name }}"
```

```
        state: started

    - name: Print OS information
      debug:
        msg: "The operating system is {{
ansible_facts['distribution'] }} {{
ansible_facts['distribution_version'] }}"
```

Save the changes, close the text editor and execute the playbook using the **ansible-playbook** command:

```
ansible-playbook
~/GitforGits/playbooks/variables_playbook.yml
```

After running the playbook, check the output to see if the package was installed, the service started, and the OS information was printed:

```
ssh user@web1.gitforgits.com

dpkg -l | grep nginx

sudo systemctl status nginx
```

With this, you have successfully used variables and facts in an Ansible playbook. This allows for more flexible and dynamic playbooks, enabling you to adapt to different environments and requirements efficiently. Understanding and utilizing variables and facts is essential for creating robust and adaptable automation scripts.

Recipe #3: Implementing Conditionals in Playbooks

Understand Conditional Statements

Implementing conditionals in Ansible playbooks allows you to execute tasks based on specific criteria or conditions. Conditional statements are defined using the **when** keyword. These conditions can evaluate variables, facts, or other criteria to determine whether a task should run. This adds flexibility to your automation scripts, enabling them to respond dynamically to different situations.

In this recipe, you will learn to implement conditionals in Ansible playbooks to execute tasks based on specific conditions. To begin with, create a new playbook file to practice implementing conditionals:

```
nano ~/GitforGits/playbooks/conditionals_playbook.yml
```

Define Variables and Tasks with Conditions

In the playbook, define tasks that only run if certain conditions are met. Given below is an example where tasks depend on the operating system:

```
---

- name: Implementing Conditionals

  hosts: webservers

  become: yes

  vars:

    package_name: nginx

  tasks:

    - name: Install Nginx on Debian-based systems

      apt:

        name: "{{ package_name }}"

        state: present

      when: ansible_facts['os_family'] == "Debian"
```

```
    - name: Install Nginx on RedHat-based systems
      yum:
        name: "{{ package_name }}"
        state: present
      when: ansible_facts['os_family'] == "RedHat"

    - name: Ensure Nginx is running
      service:
        name: nginx
        state: started
```

Save the changes and close the text editor. After running the playbook, verify that the tasks were executed correctly based on the conditions. Check if Nginx is installed and running on both Debian-based and RedHat-based systems:

```
ssh user@web1.gitforgits.com
dpkg -l | grep nginx
sudo systemctl status nginx

ssh user@web2.gitforgits.com
rpm -qa | grep nginx
sudo systemctl status nginx
```

This approach ensures that tasks are executed only when specific criteria are met, adding flexibility and precision to your automation scripts.

Recipe #4: Looping over Tasks

Looping over tasks in Ansible playbooks is a powerful feature that allows you to execute a task multiple times with different inputs. This capability is essential when you need to perform repetitive actions efficiently, such as installing multiple packages, creating several user accounts, or configuring various services. By using loops, you can avoid duplicating code and make your playbooks more concise and maintainable.

In this recipe, you will learn to loop over tasks in Ansible playbooks, enhancing the efficiency and readability of your automation scripts.

Understand Looping Constructs

Ansible provides several ways to implement loops in playbooks, with the most common method being the **loop** keyword. This keyword allows you to iterate over a list of items and execute the task for each item.

Now, create a new playbook file to practice looping over tasks:

```
nano ~/GitforGits/playbooks/loops_playbook.yml
```

Define Tasks with Loops

In the playbook, define tasks that use the **loop** keyword to perform repetitive actions. Given below is an example where multiple packages are installed using a loop:

```
---

- name: Looping Over Tasks

  hosts: webservers

  become: yes

  vars:

    packages:

      - nginx

      - git

      - curl
```

```
  tasks:
    - name: Install multiple packages
      apt:
        name: "{{ item }}"
        state: present
      loop: "{{ packages }}"
```

An alternative way to loop over items is by using **with_items**. This method is being deprecated in favor of **loop**, but it's still widely used in existing playbooks:

```
---
- name: Looping Over Tasks with with_items
  hosts: webservers
  become: yes
  vars:
    services:
      - nginx
      - apache2
  tasks:
    - name: Ensure services are running
      service:
        name: "{{ item }}"
        state: started
```

```
      with_items: "{{ services }}"
```

After running the playbook, verify that the packages were installed and services started on the target hosts:

```
ssh user@web1.gitforgits.com

dpkg -l | grep -E 'nginx|git|curl'

sudo systemctl status nginx

sudo systemctl status apache2
```

With this, you have successfully implemented loops in an Ansible playbook. Using loops reduces redundancy and simplifies your playbooks, making them easier to read and maintain, and it is particularly useful when dealing with repetitive tasks.

Recipe #5: Debugging Playbook Errors

Debugging playbook errors is a crucial skill for ensuring your Ansible automation scripts run smoothly. Understanding how to identify and fix issues can save time and prevent disruptions in your automation workflows.

In this recipe, we will teach you how to effectively debug and resolve errors in Ansible playbooks, enhancing the reliability and performance of your automation scripts.

Use --check and --diff Options

Ansible provides options to test playbooks without making actual changes. The **--check** option performs a dry run, while the **--diff** option shows changes that would be made:

```
ansible-playbook
~/GitforGits/playbooks/loops_playbook.yml --check --diff
```

This command simulates the playbook execution, helping you identify potential issues without altering your systems.

Enable Verbose Mode

Verbose mode provides detailed output, making it easier to pinpoint errors. Use the **-v**, **-vv**, or -

vvv options to increase verbosity:

```
ansible-playbook
~/GitforGits/playbooks/loops_playbook.yml -vv
```

Verbose output includes detailed information about task execution, which can help you understand where and why errors occur.

Use the debug Module

The **debug** module allows you to print variable values and custom messages during playbook execution. This is helpful for understanding the state of your environment and troubleshooting issues:

```
---

- name: Debugging Playbook

  hosts: webservers

  become: yes

  vars:

    packages:

      - nginx

      - git

      - curl

  tasks:

    - name: Install multiple packages

      apt:

        name: "{{ item }}"

        state: present
```

```
      loop: "{{ packages }}"


    - name: Print variable value
      debug:
        msg: "Package being installed: {{ item }}"
      loop: "{{ packages }}"
```

Check Return Codes and Standard Output

Ansible modules return detailed information about task execution. Capture and inspect this information to debug issues:

```
- name: Capture command output
  command: ls /nonexistent
  register: result


- name: Print command output
  debug:
    var: result
```

The **register** keyword stores the output of a task, and the **debug** module prints it, allowing you to analyze the results and diagnose problems.

Review Playbook Logs

Ansible logs provide valuable insights into playbook execution. Check the logs to understand the sequence of events leading up to an error:

```
tail -f /var/log/ansible.log
```

Ensure that logging is enabled in your **ansible.cfg** file:

```
[defaults]

log_path = /var/log/ansible.log
```

Correcting Common Errors

- Ensure YAML syntax is correct, such as proper indentation and correct use of colons and dashes.
- Verify module arguments and ensure they are correctly specified.
- Check SSH connectivity and authentication issues.
- Ensure variables are correctly defined and referenced.

Rerun the Playbook

After identifying and correcting errors, rerun the playbook to verify that the issues are resolved:

```
ansible-playbook
~/GitforGits/playbooks/loops_playbook.yml
```

Now, you have learned how to debug and resolve errors in Ansible playbooks. This ensures that your automation scripts run smoothly and reliably, reducing downtime and improving overall efficiency.

Recipe #6: Using Handlers for Task Notifications

Handlers are special tasks that are triggered by other tasks when a change occurs. They are typically used to perform actions that should only happen if something has changed, such as restarting a service after a configuration file has been modified. Handlers help ensure that these actions are only taken when necessary, improving the efficiency and reliability of your playbooks.

In this recipe, you will learn to use handlers in Ansible playbooks to perform tasks based on notifications from other tasks.

Understand Handlers

Handlers are defined in the same way as regular tasks but are placed under a **handlers** section. A task can notify one or more handlers if it changes the state of the system. Handlers are run at the end of a play, ensuring that all necessary changes are made before any dependent actions are taken.

To begin with, create a new playbook file to practice using handlers:

```
nano ~/GitforGits/playbooks/handlers_playbook.yml
```

Define Tasks and Handlers

In the playbook, define tasks that notify handlers when changes occur. Given below is an example where a handler restarts the Nginx service if the configuration file is modified:

```
---

- name: Using Handlers

  hosts: webservers

  become: yes

  tasks:

    - name: Ensure Nginx is installed

      apt:

        name: nginx

        state: present


    - name: Copy Nginx configuration file

      copy:

        src: /path/to/local/nginx.conf

        dest: /etc/nginx/nginx.conf

        owner: root

        group: root
```

```
        mode: '0644'
      notify:
        - Restart Nginx

  handlers:
    - name: Restart Nginx
      service:
        name: nginx
        state: restarted
```

Save the changes, close the text editor and execute the playbook using the **ansible-playbook** command. After running the playbook, verify that the Nginx service was restarted if the configuration file was changed:

```
ssh user@web1.gitforgits.com
sudo systemctl status nginx
```

The output should show that the Nginx service was restarted if the configuration file was modified.

Handlers can also be used for various tasks beyond restarting services. Given below are a few advanced use cases:

- **Reloading Services:** Handlers can be used to reload services, ensuring new configurations are applied without a full restart.
- **Running Scripts:** Handlers can trigger custom scripts to perform additional setup or cleanup tasks.
- **Combining Handlers:** Multiple tasks can notify the same handler, allowing a single action to be taken based on multiple conditions.

By following these steps, you have learned how to use handlers in Ansible playbooks to perform task notifications. Handlers ensure that actions are only taken when necessary, making your playbooks more efficient and reliable.

Recipe #7: Organizing Playbooks with Includes and Imports

Organizing playbooks with includes and imports helps you manage complex automation tasks by breaking down large playbooks into smaller, reusable components. This approach enhances readability, maintainability, and reusability of your automation code. Includes and imports allow you to include tasks, variables, handlers, and other playbook components from separate files, making it easier to structure and manage your Ansible projects.

Significance of Includes and Imports

- **Modularity:** Breaking down playbooks into smaller files makes them easier to manage and understand.
- **Reusability:** Reusable components can be included in multiple playbooks, reducing duplication.
- **Maintainability:** Smaller, focused files are easier to maintain and update.
- **Readability:** Clear, organized playbooks are easier to read and follow, especially for complex automation tasks.

In this recipe, you will learn to use includes and imports in Ansible playbooks to create modular and organized automation scripts.

Understanding Includes and Imports

- **`include_tasks`** allows you to include a task file at runtime. It is dynamic and does not require the playbook to be re-parsed.
- **`import_tasks`** includes a task file at parse time, making it static. It is parsed when the playbook starts running.
- **`include_playbook`** allows you to include an entire playbook at runtime.
- **`import_playbook`** includes an entire playbook at parse time.

Create the Task Files

Create a directory for task files and add a sample task file:

```
mkdir ~/GitforGits/playbooks/tasks

nano ~/GitforGits/playbooks/tasks/install_packages.yml
```

Add the given below script to the task file:

```
---
- name: Install Nginx
  apt:
    name: nginx
    state: present

- name: Install Git
  apt:
    name: git
    state: present
```

Create Main Playbook File

Create a new playbook file that uses includes and imports:

```
nano ~/GitforGits/playbooks/main_playbook.yml
```

Add the given below script to include the tasks:

```
---
- name: Main Playbook with Includes and Imports
  hosts: webservers
  become: yes
  tasks:
    - name: Include install_packages tasks
```

```
    include_tasks: tasks/install_packages.yml

  - name: Include setup_handlers
    include_tasks: tasks/setup_handlers.yml
```

Create Additional Task Files

Create another task file for handlers:

```
nano ~/GitforGits/playbooks/tasks/setup_handlers.yml
```

Add the script as given below:

```
---
- name: Ensure Nginx is running
  service:
    name: nginx
    state: started

- name: Ensure Git is installed
  command: git --version
```

After running the playbook, verify that the packages were installed and services started on the target hosts:

```
ssh user@web1.gitforgits.com
dpkg -l | grep nginx
dpkg -l | grep git
```

```
sudo systemctl status nginx

git --version
```

With these steps, you have learned how to organize playbooks with includes and imports in Ansible and also this approach enhances the modularity, reusability, and maintainability of your automation scripts, making it easier to manage complex automation tasks efficiently.

Recipe #8: Running Playbooks Across Multiple Machines

Running playbooks across multiple machines is a fundamental aspect of Ansible's power in managing large-scale infrastructures. This capability allows you to automate tasks simultaneously on multiple hosts, ensuring consistency and efficiency in your configurations and deployments. It is essential for scenarios such as rolling out updates, applying security patches, configuring services, and deploying applications across a fleet of servers.

Necessity of Running Playbooks Across Multiple Machines

- **Consistency:** Ensures all machines are configured uniformly, reducing configuration drift.
- **Efficiency:** Automates repetitive tasks across many hosts, saving time and effort.
- **Scalability:** Manages infrastructure at scale, allowing for the automation of hundreds or thousands of servers.
- **Reliability:** Reduces the risk of human error by automating complex and repetitive tasks.

In this recipe, you will learn to run Ansible playbooks across multiple machines to manage and automate tasks efficiently.

Define Inventory Groups

Ensure your inventory file categorizes the machines into groups:

```
nano ~/GitforGits/inventory/hosts
```

Organize your hosts into groups:

```
[webservers]
```

```
web1.gitforgits.com
web2.gitforgits.com

[databases]
db1.gitforgits.com
db2.gitforgits.com
```

Again, create a new playbook file to practice running tasks across multiple machines:

```
nano ~/GitforGits/playbooks/multi_machine_playbook.yml
```

Define Tasks for Multiple Groups

In the playbook, define tasks that target multiple groups of machines:

```
---
- name: Configure Web Servers
  hosts: webservers
  become: yes
  tasks:
    - name: Ensure Nginx is installed
      apt:
        name: nginx
        state: present

    - name: Start Nginx service
```

```
      service:
        name: nginx
        state: started

- name: Configure Database Servers
  hosts: databases
  become: yes
  tasks:
    - name: Ensure MySQL is installed
      apt:
        name: mysql-server
        state: present
    - name: Start MySQL service
      service:
        name: mysql
        state: started
```

After running the playbook, verify that the tasks were executed correctly on all target hosts:

```
ssh user@web1.gitforgits.com
dpkg -l | grep nginx
sudo systemctl status nginx
```

```
ssh user@web2.gitforgits.com

dpkg -l | grep nginx

sudo systemctl status nginx


ssh user@db1.gitforgits.com

dpkg -l | grep mysql-server

sudo systemctl status mysql


ssh user@db2.gitforgits.com

dpkg -l | grep mysql-server

sudo systemctl status mysql
```

These steps made possible to run Ansible playbooks across multiple machines. This approach is essential for managing large-scale infrastructures efficiently, ensuring consistent configurations and streamlined automation processes across your entire environment.

Summary

In this chapter, you learned the fundamentals of Ansible playbook creation and execution, beginning with the creation of your first playbook. You learned about remote host facts and variables, which allowed you to create dynamic and adaptable playbooks. The implementation of conditionals enabled the execution of tasks based on specific criteria, thereby increasing the flexibility of your automation scripts. Looping over tasks is a skill that you acquired, enabling you to perform repetitive tasks without the need to duplicate code. The debug module, verbose mode, --check, and --diff were all utilized to identify and resolve playbook errors. Also addressed were the methods of debugging. To maximize the efficiency of the playbook, task notification handlers were used to make sure that actions like service restarts only happened when absolutely needed. It was shown how to organize playbooks using imports and includes, which allows for better readability and maintainability by separating big playbooks into multiple modular components. Ultimately, you executed playbooks on multiple machines, simultaneously managing and automating tasks on various hosts to guarantee the consistency and efficiency of your configurations.

When you put what you've learned from both chapters into practice, you'll be well-equipped to create Ansible environments, configure them, and write effective playbooks. The initial chapter addressed the following topics: the installation of Ansible, the configuration of control nodes, the initialization of projects, the establishment of SSH key-based authentication, the organization of directory structures, the management of configuration files, the establishment of a local virtual development environment, and the connection to remote hosts. These abilities, when combined with the playbook writing techniques outlined in this chapter, allow you to automate intricate tasks, manage infrastructure at a large scale, and ensure that your systems are configured consistently and reliably.

Knowledge Exercise

Question 1: What is the primary purpose of a playbook in Ansible?
A) To install Ansible
B) To define a set of tasks to be executed on specified hosts
C) To manage Ansible configuration files
D) To set up SSH key-based authentication

Answer:
B) To define a set of tasks to be executed on specified hosts

Playbooks are YAML files that describe tasks Ansible should run on specified hosts, forming the core of Ansible's automation capabilities.

Question 2: How are variables defined in an Ansible playbook?
A) Under the **tasks** section
B) In a separate file
C) Under the **vars** section
D) In the inventory file

Answer:
C) Under the **vars** section

Variables can be defined directly within a playbook under the **vars** section, allowing for dynamic and reusable values in tasks.

Question 3: Which module is used to gather facts about remote hosts in Ansible?
A) **setup**
B) **gather_facts**

C) **collect_facts**
D) **fetch_facts**

Answer:
A) **setup**

The **setup** module automatically gathers facts about remote hosts, providing detailed information that can be used within playbooks.

Question 4: What keyword is used to implement conditionals in Ansible playbooks?
A) **if**
B) **when**
C) **conditional**
D) **unless**

Answer:
B) **when**

The **when** keyword is used to implement conditionals in Ansible playbooks, allowing tasks to run based on specific criteria.

Question 5: Which option allows you to simulate the execution of a playbook without making any changes?
A) **--dry-run**
B) **--simulate**
C) **--check**
D) **--test**

Answer:
C) **--check**

The **--check** option performs a dry run, simulating the execution of a playbook without making any actual changes to the systems.

Question 6: What is the primary function of the **debug** module in Ansible playbooks?
A) To install debug tools
B) To print variable values and custom messages
C) To gather system logs
D) To restart services

Answer:

B) To print variable values and custom messages

The **debug** module is used to print variable values and custom messages, helping troubleshoot and understand playbook execution.

Question 7: How are handlers defined in an Ansible playbook?
A) Under the **tasks** section
B) Under the **vars** section
C) Under the **handlers** section
D) In the inventory file

Answer:
C) Under the **handlers** section

Handlers are defined under the **handlers** section in a playbook and are triggered by other tasks when changes occur.

Question 8: Which keyword is used to include task files at runtime in Ansible playbooks?
A) **import_tasks**
B) **include_tasks**
C) **include**
D) **import**

Answer:
B) **include_tasks**

The **include_tasks** keyword is used to include task files at runtime, allowing for dynamic inclusion of tasks.

Question 9: What is the advantage of using **loop** in Ansible playbooks?
A) It speeds up playbook execution
B) It allows tasks to be executed multiple times with different inputs
C) It simplifies playbook syntax
D) It reduces the number of hosts

Answer:
B) It allows tasks to be executed multiple times with different inputs

Using **loop** in Ansible playbooks allows tasks to be executed multiple times with different inputs, making playbooks more efficient and readable.

Question 10: What command is used to run an Ansible playbook on specified hosts?
A) **ansible**
B) **ansible-playbook**
C) **ansible-run**
D) **ansible-execute**

Answer:
B) **ansible-playbook**

The **ansible-playbook** command is used to run an Ansible playbook on specified hosts, executing the tasks defined in the playbook.

Question 11: How can you ensure a task only runs on Debian-based systems using conditionals?
A) **when: ansible_os_family == "Debian"**
B) **when: ansible_facts['os_family'] == "Debian"**
C) **if: ansible_os_family == "Debian"**
D) **unless: ansible_os_family == "Debian"**

Answer:
B) **when: ansible_facts['os_family'] == "Debian"**

To ensure a task only runs on Debian-based systems, use the **when** keyword with the fact **ansible_facts['os_family']**.

Question 12: Which command provides detailed output during playbook execution for debugging purposes?
A) **ansible-playbook -d**
B) **ansible-playbook -v**
C) **ansible-playbook -vv**
D) **ansible-playbook --debug**

Answer:
C) **ansible-playbook -vv**

Using **ansible-playbook -vv** increases verbosity, providing detailed output that is useful for debugging.

Question 13: What section of a playbook is used to define reusable sets of tasks?
A) **vars**
B) **roles**

C) **tasks**
D) **handlers**

Answer:
B) **roles**

The **roles** section is used to define reusable sets of tasks, making playbooks modular and maintainable.

Question 14: How do you print the value of a variable during playbook execution?
A) Using the **print** module
B) Using the **display** module
C) Using the **debug** module
D) Using the **echo** module

Answer:
C) Using the **debug** module

The **debug** module is used to print the value of a variable during playbook execution, helping to understand and troubleshoot the playbook.

Question 15: Which keyword is used to notify a handler to execute after a task has changed?
A) **alert**
B) **trigger**
C) **notify**
D) **signal**

Answer:
C) **notify**

The **notify** keyword is used to notify a handler to execute after a task has changed, ensuring dependent actions are taken only when necessary.

Question 16: What is the purpose of the **import_tasks** keyword in Ansible playbooks?
A) To include tasks at runtime
B) To include tasks at parse time
C) To import variables
D) To import inventory files

Answer:
B) To include tasks at parse time

The **import_tasks** keyword includes tasks at parse time, making it static and parsed when the playbook starts running.

Question 17: Which command can be used to test a playbook without making any changes?
A) **ansible-playbook --dry-run**
B) **ansible-playbook --simulate**
C) **ansible-playbook --check**
D) **ansible-playbook --test**

Answer:
C) **ansible-playbook --check**

The **--check** option simulates the execution of a playbook without making any actual changes, helping to identify potential issues.

Question 18: How do you ensure that a service is restarted only if a configuration file changes?
A) Use the **restart** module
B) Define a handler and use **notify**
C) Use the **changed_when** keyword
D) Use the **conditional** keyword

Answer:
B) Define a handler and use **notify**

To ensure a service is restarted only if a configuration file changes, define a handler and use the **notify** keyword to trigger the handler when the task changes.

Question 19: What is the benefit of organizing playbooks with includes and imports?
A) It speeds up playbook execution
B) It makes playbooks more modular and maintainable
C) It simplifies playbook syntax
D) It reduces the number of tasks

Answer:
B) It makes playbooks more modular and maintainable

Organizing playbooks with includes and imports makes them more modular and maintainable, allowing for reusable components and better organization.

Question 20: How do you specify a list of items to loop over in an Ansible playbook?
A) Using the **list** keyword

B) Using the **for** keyword
C) Using the **loop** keyword
D) Using the **iterate** keyword

Answer:
C) Using the **loop** keyword

The **loop** keyword is used to specify a list of items to iterate over in an Ansible playbook, making tasks more efficient and readable.

CHAPTER 3: MANAGING INVENTORIES

Introduction

As you recall from the last chapter, Ansible playbooks are a powerful tool for automating tasks with the help of variables, conditionals, loops, and handlers. You concurrently studied the organization of playbooks with imports and includes and the execution of these playbooks across multiple machines.

Inventory management is covered in detail in this chapter. First, you will establish static inventories, which are a straightforward and uncomplicated approach to compiling a list of hosts. Subsequently, you will proceed to develop dynamic inventories that can automatically generate host lists by utilizing external data sources. Additionally, you are going to learn the utilization of inventory plugins to integrate with a variety of external systems and services.

You will acquire the knowledge necessary to effectively define and utilize these groups, which enables more organized and scalable management by grouping hosts in inventories. By utilizing host and group variables, it is possible to customize configurations to correspond with particular hosts or groups. Additionally, you will acquire the knowledge necessary to effectively manage inventory files with Git, which will guarantee collaboration and version control. Lastly, you will be prepared to handle typical issues that arise during inventory management by learning how to troubleshoot inventory issues.

At the chapter's conclusion, you will have a clear understanding of how to structure and identify the hosts that your playbooks will automate.

Recipe #1: Setting up Static Inventories

Inventories are essential for defining the hosts and groups of hosts that Ansible will manage. An inventory file lists the managed nodes and groups them into categories, allowing you to target specific hosts or groups with your playbooks. This structured approach helps Ansible users manage large infrastructures efficiently by organizing hosts in a clear and scalable manner.

Purpose of Inventory

- **Host Management:** Inventories list all the hosts managed by Ansible, making it easy to target specific machines.
- **Grouping:** Hosts can be grouped based on roles, environments, or any logical categorization, simplifying the execution of tasks on related hosts.
- **Variable Assignment:** Inventories allow for the assignment of variables to hosts and groups, enabling customized configurations for different parts of the infrastructure.
- **Scalability:** By organizing hosts into groups, Ansible can manage large-scale environments more effectively.

Types of Inventories

- **Static Inventories:** These are simple text files where hosts and groups are listed manually. They are straightforward but require manual updates.
- **Dynamic Inventories:** These are generated dynamically based on external data sources such as cloud provider APIs, CMDBs, or other services. They automatically update the list of hosts, making them ideal for dynamic environments.

In this recipe, you will learn to set up a static inventory, providing a foundation for managing hosts and groups in a straightforward and organized manner.

Create Inventory File

Create a directory for your inventory files if you haven't already:

```
mkdir ~/GitforGits/inventory
```

Create a new static inventory file:

```
nano ~/GitforGits/inventory/hosts
```

Define Hosts and Groups

List your hosts and organize them into groups. Given below is an example inventory file:

```
[webservers]

web1.gitforgits.com

web2.gitforgits.com


[databases]

db1.gitforgits.com

db2.gitforgits.com
```

```
[all:vars]
ansible_user=your_user
ansible_ssh_private_key_file=~/.ssh/id_rsa
```

In the above code snippet,

- Hosts are categorized into **`webservers`** and **`databases`** groups.
- Variables common to all hosts are defined under **`[all:vars]`**.

Ensure your Ansible configuration points to the correct inventory file. Open the **ansible.cfg** file:

```
nano ~/GitforGits/ansible.cfg
```

Add or update the inventory path:

```
[defaults]
inventory = inventory/hosts
```

Verify the Inventory

Test the inventory to ensure it's correctly set up. Use the **ansible-inventory** command to list all hosts:

```
ansible-inventory --list -y
```

This command should display a structured output of your inventory, confirming that Ansible can read and interpret it correctly.

Use Inventory in a Playbook

Create a playbook to test the inventory setup:

```
nano ~/GitforGits/playbooks/test_inventory.yml
```

Add the script as given below:

```
---
- name: Test Inventory
  hosts: all
  tasks:
    - name: Ping all hosts
      ping:
```

Execute the playbook to verify that Ansible can connect to all hosts listed in the inventory:

```
ansible-playbook
~/GitforGits/playbooks/test_inventory.yml
```

By following these steps, you have successfully set up a static inventory. This setup allows you to manage and organize your hosts effectively, providing a foundation for executing playbooks across different groups and environments. Static inventories are simple and straightforward, making them ideal for smaller or more static infrastructures.

Recipe #2: Creating Dynamic Inventories

Dynamic inventories allow you to automatically generate and update the list of hosts based on external data sources. This is particularly useful for managing dynamic environments, such as cloud infrastructure, where hosts are frequently added or removed. Dynamic inventories help ensure that your inventory is always up-to-date without requiring manual updates.

Purpose and Benefits of Dynamic Inventories

- **Automation:** Automatically updates the list of hosts, reducing the need for manual intervention.
- **Scalability:** Ideal for large and dynamic environments where hosts are frequently changing.
- **Integration:** Can integrate with cloud providers, CMDBs, and other external data sources to pull host information.
- **Consistency:** Ensures the inventory is always in sync with the actual infrastructure.

In this recipe, you will learn to create and use dynamic inventories, leveraging external data sources to manage hosts efficiently.

Install boto3

Depending on your environment, you may need to install additional packages or plugins. For example, to use AWS as a dynamic inventory source, you need the **boto3** package:

```
pip install boto3
```

Create Dynamic Inventory Script

Dynamic inventories can be created using custom scripts or plugins. For AWS, you can use the AWS EC2 inventory plugin. Create a new configuration file for the plugin:

```
mkdir -p ~/GitforGits/inventory/aws_ec2

nano ~/GitforGits/inventory/aws_ec2/aws_ec2.yml
```

Add the given below script to configure the AWS EC2 inventory plugin:

```
plugin: aws_ec2

regions:

  - us-east-1

  - us-west-2

filters:

  instance-state-name: running

keyed_groups:

  - key: tags.Name

    prefix: tag

hostnames:

  - tag:Name
```

```
compose:
  ansible_host: public_ip_address
```

This configuration specifies the regions, filters instances by their running state, and organizes hosts by their tags.

Update Ansible Configuration

Ensure your **ansible.cfg** file points to the dynamic inventory configuration:

```
nano ~/GitforGits/ansible.cfg
```

Add or update the inventory path:

```
[defaults]
inventory = inventory/aws_ec2/aws_ec2.yml
```

Verify Dynamic Inventory

Test the dynamic inventory to ensure it's correctly set up. Use the **ansible-inventory** command to list all hosts:

```
ansible-inventory --list -y
```

This command should display the dynamic inventory generated from AWS, confirming that Ansible can read and interpret it correctly.

Use Dynamic Inventory in a Playbook

Create a playbook to test the dynamic inventory setup:

```
nano ~/GitforGits/playbooks/test_dynamic_inventory.yml
```

Copy the following:

```
---
```

```
- name: Test Dynamic Inventory
  hosts: all
  tasks:
    - name: Ping all hosts
      ping:
```

Execute the playbook to verify that Ansible can connect to all hosts listed in the dynamic inventory:

```
ansible-playbook
~/GitforGits/playbooks/test_dynamic_inventory.yml
```

Dynamic inventories can also be extended and customized to suit various environments. Following are some additional use cases:

- **Using Other Cloud Providers:** Similar plugins are available for other cloud providers like Azure, Google Cloud, and OpenStack.
- **Custom Scripts:** You can create custom scripts to pull inventory data from databases, REST APIs, or other sources.
- **Combining Inventories:** Ansible supports combining static and dynamic inventories to manage different parts of your infrastructure effectively.

Recipe #3: Using Inventory Plugins

Inventory plugins are used to dynamically generate inventory from various sources, such as cloud providers, CMDBs, and other external systems. These plugins are beneficial when managing dynamic environments where hosts are frequently added or removed. Inventory plugins help automate the inventory management process, ensuring that your inventory is always up-to-date and in sync with the actual infrastructure.

In this recipe, you will learn to use Ansible inventory plugins to dynamically generate and manage inventory from external sources.

Install Azure

Depending on the inventory plugin you plan to use, you may need to install additional packages. For example, to use the Azure inventory plugin, install the **azure** package:

```
pip install azure
```

Configure Inventory Plugin

Create a directory for the inventory plugin configuration and add the necessary configuration files. For this example, we will use the AWS EC2 inventory plugin. If not already created in Recipe #2, create the configuration file:

```
mkdir -p ~/GitforGits/inventory/aws_ec2

nano ~/GitforGits/inventory/aws_ec2/aws_ec2.yml
```

Add the given below script to configure the AWS EC2 inventory plugin:

```
plugin: aws_ec2

regions:

  - us-east-1

  - us-west-2

filters:

  instance-state-name: running

keyed_groups:

  - key: tags.Name

    prefix: tag

hostnames:

  - tag:Name

compose:

  ansible_host: public_ip_address
```

This configuration specifies the AWS regions to query, filters instances by their running state, and organizes hosts by their tags.

Now, ensure your **ansible.cfg** file points to the inventory plugin configuration:

```
nano ~/GitforGits/ansible.cfg
```

Add or update the inventory path:

```
[defaults]

inventory = inventory/aws_ec2/aws_ec2.yml
```

Test the inventory plugin to ensure it's correctly set up. Use the **ansible-inventory** command to list all hosts:

```
ansible-inventory --list -y
```

This command should display the dynamic inventory generated by the AWS EC2 plugin, confirming that Ansible can read and interpret it correctly.

Create a playbook to test the inventory plugin setup:

```
nano ~/GitforGits/playbooks/test_inventory_plugin.yml
```

Copy the following:

```
---

- name: Test Inventory Plugin

  hosts: all

  tasks:

    - name: Ping all hosts

      ping:
```

Execute the playbook to verify that Ansible can connect to all hosts listed by the inventory plugin:

```
ansible-playbook
~/GitforGits/playbooks/test_inventory_plugin.yml
```

Inventory plugins also can be customized to fit various environmentssuch as to:

- Combine multiple inventory plugins to pull data from different sources, such as combining AWS and Azure inventories.
- Develop custom inventory plugins to integrate with proprietary systems or databases.
- Use parameters to filter and organize hosts dynamically, based on tags, states, or other attributes.

Recipe #4: Grouping Hosts in Inventories

Grouping hosts categorizes hosts into logical groups, you can target specific sets of machines with your playbooks, making it easier to apply configurations, updates, and tasks consistently across similar hosts. Grouping hosts also enhances scalability and maintainability, as it simplifies the process of managing large-scale environments.

Benefits of Grouping Hosts

- Run playbooks on specific groups of hosts, such as web servers, databases, or application servers.
- Easier to manage configurations and tasks for large numbers of hosts by addressing groups rather than individual machines.
- Ensure consistent configurations and updates across all hosts in a group.
- Dynamically adjust groups as your infrastructure changes, adding or removing hosts as needed.

In this recipe, you will learn to group hosts in Ansible inventories, allowing you to organize and manage your infrastructure efficiently.

Define Host Groups

Open the inventory file and then group your hosts based on their roles or any logical categorization that fits your infrastructure. Following is an example inventory file:

```
[webservers]

web1.gitforgits.com
```

```
web2.gitforgits.com


[databases]

db1.gitforgits.com

db2.gitforgits.com


[loadbalancers]

lb1.gitforgits.com

lb2.gitforgits.com
```

In the above code snippet,

- **`webservers`** group includes all web servers.
- **`databases`** group includes all database servers.
- **`loadbalancers`** group includes all load balancers.

Use Group Variables

You can assign variables to specific groups to customize configurations for different sets of hosts. Add group variables to the inventory file:

```
[webservers]

web1.gitforgits.com

web2.gitforgits.com


[databases]

db1.gitforgits.com
```

```
db2.gitforgits.com
[loadbalancers]
lb1.gitforgits.com
lb2.gitforgits.com

[webservers:vars]
http_port=80
max_clients=200

[databases:vars]
db_port=3306
db_user=admin
db_password=secret

[loadbalancers:vars]
balancer_algorithm=round-robin
```

Use Host Groups

Create a new playbook file to demonstrate how to target specific groups:

```
nano ~/GitforGits/playbooks/grouping_hosts_playbook.yml
```

Add the given below script to target the **webservers** and **databases** groups with different tasks:

```
---
```

```yaml
- name: Configure Web Servers
  hosts: webservers
  become: yes
  tasks:
    - name: Ensure Nginx is installed
      apt:
        name: nginx
        state: present

    - name: Configure Nginx
      template:
        src: /path/to/nginx.conf.j2
        dest: /etc/nginx/nginx.conf
      notify:
        - Restart Nginx

  handlers:
    - name: Restart Nginx
      service:
        name: nginx
        state: restarted
```

```yaml
- name: Configure Database Servers
  hosts: databases
  become: yes
  tasks:
    - name: Ensure MySQL is installed
      apt:
        name: mysql-server
        state: present

    - name: Configure MySQL
      template:
        src: /path/to/my.cnf.j2
        dest: /etc/mysql/my.cnf
      notify:
        - Restart MySQL

  handlers:
    - name: Restart MySQL
      service:
        name: mysql
```

```
        state: restarted
```

After running the playbook, verify that the tasks were executed correctly on all target hosts:

```
ssh user@web1.gitforgits.com

dpkg -l | grep nginx

sudo systemctl status nginx


ssh user@db1.gitforgits.com

dpkg -l | grep mysql-server

sudo systemctl status mysql
```

This technique helps you manage your infrastructure more efficiently, ensuring consistency and simplifying the process of targeting specific sets of machines with your playbooks and is also vital for maintaining organized and scalable automation workflows.

Recipe #5: Working with Host and Group Variables

Host and group variables provide a powerful way to customize configurations for specific hosts or groups of hosts. These variables can be defined directly in the inventory file or in separate variable files, allowing for flexible and dynamic configuration management. In this recipe, you will learn to define and use host and group variables, enabling customized configurations for your infrastructure.

Add the given below script in the inventory file to define variables for specific hosts and groups:

```
[webservers]

web1.gitforgits.com

web2.gitforgits.com
```

```
[databases]
db1.gitforgits.com
db2.gitforgits.com

[webservers:vars]
http_port=80
max_clients=200

[databases:vars]
db_port=3306
db_user=admin
db_password=secret

[web1.gitforgits.com]
ansible_host=192.168.1.10

[db1.gitforgits.com]
ansible_host=192.168.1.20
```

Create Separate Variable Files

For better organization, you can define variables in separate files within **group_vars** and **host_vars** directories. Create these directories if they don't exist:

```
mkdir -p ~/GitforGits/inventory/group_vars
mkdir -p ~/GitforGits/inventory/host_vars
```

Create a group variable file for web servers:

```
nano ~/GitforGits/inventory/group_vars/webservers.yml
```

Copy the following:

```
http_port: 80
max_clients: 200
```

Create a group variable file for databases:

```
nano ~/GitforGits/inventory/group_vars/databases.yml
```

Copy the following:

```
db_port: 3306
db_user: admin
db_password: secret
```

Create a host variable file for **web1.gitforgits.com**:

```
nano
~/GitforGits/inventory/host_vars/web1.gitforgits.com.yml
```

Copy the following:

```
ansible_host: 192.168.1.10
```

Create a host variable file for **db1.gitforgits.com**:

```
nano
~/GitforGits/inventory/host_vars/db1.gitforgits.com.yml
```

Add the following code snippet:

```
ansible_host: 192.168.1.20
```

Use Variables in a Playbook

Create a new playbook file to demonstrate how to use host and group variables:

```
nano ~/GitforGits/playbooks/host_group_vars_playbook.yml
```

Copy the following:

```
---

- name: Configure Web Servers

  hosts: webservers

  become: yes

  tasks:

    - name: Ensure Nginx is installed

      apt:

        name: nginx

        state: present


    - name: Configure Nginx

      template:

        src: /path/to/nginx.conf.j2
```

```
        dest: /etc/nginx/nginx.conf
      notify:
        - Restart Nginx

  handlers:
    - name: Restart Nginx
      service:
        name: nginx
        state: restarted

- name: Configure Database Servers
  hosts: databases
  become: yes
  tasks:
    - name: Ensure MySQL is installed
      apt:
        name: mysql-server
        state: present

    - name: Configure MySQL
      template:
```

```
        src: /path/to/my.cnf.j2
        dest: /etc/mysql/my.cnf
      notify:
        - Restart MySQL

  handlers:
    - name: Restart MySQL
      service:
        name: mysql
        state: restarted
```

After running the playbook, verify that the variables were applied:

```
ssh user@web1.gitforgits.com
curl -I localhost:80

ssh user@db1.gitforgits.com
mysql -uadmin -psecret -e "SHOW DATABASES;"
```

By following these steps, you have successfully defined and used host and group variables. Working with host and group variables enhances the flexibility and maintainability of your Ansible playbooks. This approach allows for customized configurations, ensuring that each host or group receives the appropriate settings based on its context.

Recipe #6: Managing Inventory Files with Git

Using Git to manage your Ansible inventory files provides version control, collaboration, and backup capabilities. This ensures that changes to your inventory are tracked, and you can easily revert to previous versions if needed. In this recipe, you'll learn how to install and configure Git in your development environment and use it to manage your Ansible inventory files.

In this recipe, you will learn to install and configure Git, and then use it to manage Ansible inventory files, providing version control and collaboration features.

Install and Configure Git

First, install Git on your development environment. For Debian-based systems like Ubuntu, use:

```
sudo apt update

sudo apt install git -y
```

For Red Hat-based systems like CentOS, use:

```
sudo yum install git -y
```

Verify the installation by checking the Git version:

```
git --version
```

Configure your Git user name and email, which are used for commit messages:

```
git config --global user.name "Your Name"

git config --global user.email
"your.email@gitforgits.com"
```

Initialize Git Repository and Add Inventory Files

Navigate to your Ansible project directory and initialize a new Git repository:

```
cd ~/GitforGits

git init
```

Add your inventory files to the Git repository:

```
cd inventory
git add hosts group_vars host_vars
```

Commit the added files to the repository with a descriptive message:

```
git commit -m "Initial commit of inventory files"
```

Create a Remote Repository

If you are using a remote Git service like GitHub, GitLab, or Bitbucket, create a new repository on the service. Then, add the remote repository URL to your local repository:

```
git remote add origin
https://github.com/yourusername/GitforGits.git
```

Push your local commits to the remote repository:

```
git push -u origin master
```

Collaborate and Manage Inventory Files

Now that your inventory files are under version control, you can collaborate with others, track changes, and revert to previous versions if needed. Use the following Git commands to manage your inventory files:

- See the status of your repository and any changes:

```
git status
```

- Stage changes for commit:

```
git add <file_or_directory>
```

- Commit the staged changes:

```
git commit -m "Your commit message"
```

- Pull the latest changes from the remote repository:

```
git pull origin master
```

- Push your local commits to the remote repository:

```
git push origin master
```

Git with Ansible Playbooks

Create a playbook to manage and deploy your inventory files. Given below is an example playbook that copies the inventory files from the Git repository to the Ansible directory:

```
nano ~/GitforGits/playbooks/deploy_inventory.yml
```

Copy the following:

```
---
- name: Deploy Inventory Files
  hosts: localhost
  tasks:
    - name: Ensure Git repository is cloned
      git:
        repo:
'https://github.com/yourusername/GitforGits.git'
        dest: /path/to/your/ansible/directory
        update: yes

    - name: Copy inventory files to Ansible directory
```

```
    copy:
      src: /path/to/your/ansible/directory/inventory/
      dest: /etc/ansible/
      owner: your_user
      group: your_group
      mode: '0755'
```

Execute the playbook to deploy the inventory files from the Git repository:

```
ansible-playbook
~/GitforGits/playbooks/deploy_inventory.yml
```

This setup provides version control, collaboration, and backup capabilities, ensuring that your inventory is always up-to-date and changes are tracked.

Recipe #7: Connecting to Cloud Instances with Dynamic Inventories

Using dynamic inventories with cloud providers like AWS allows you to automatically manage and update the list of hosts based on your cloud infrastructure. This recipe will demonstrate in setting up a dynamic inventory for AWS EC2 instances, enabling seamless management of cloud resources.

Our goal in this recipe is to connect to AWS cloud instances using dynamic inventories, leveraging AWS EC2 inventory plugin.

Install boto3 and botocore

Ensure you have the necessary packages installed for AWS integration. Install the **boto3** and **botocore** packages:

```
pip install boto3 botocore
```

Configure AWS Credentials

Configure your AWS credentials to allow Ansible to interact with AWS services. Create or edit the AWS credentials file:

```
mkdir -p ~/.aws

nano ~/.aws/credentials
```

Add your AWS access key and secret access key:

```
[default]

aws_access_key_id = YOUR_ACCESS_KEY

aws_secret_access_key = YOUR_SECRET_KEY
```

Create Dynamic Inventory Configuration File

Create a directory for the dynamic inventory configuration if it doesn't exist:

```
mkdir -p ~/GitforGits/inventory/aws_ec2

nano ~/GitforGits/inventory/aws_ec2/aws_ec2.yml
```

Add the given below script to configure the AWS EC2 inventory plugin:

```
plugin: aws_ec2

regions:

  - us-east-1

  - us-west-2

filters:

  instance-state-name: running

keyed_groups:

  - key: tags.Name
```

```
    prefix: tag
hostnames:
  - tag:Name
compose:
  ansible_host: public_ip_address
```

This configuration specifies the AWS regions to query, filters instances by their running state, and organizes hosts by their tags.

Update Ansible Configuration

Ensure your **ansible.cfg** file points to the dynamic inventory configuration:

```
nano ~/GitforGits/ansible.cfg
```

Add or update the inventory path:

```
[defaults]
inventory = inventory/aws_ec2/aws_ec2.yml
```

Verify Dynamic Inventory

Test the dynamic inventory to ensure it's correctly set up. Use the **ansible-inventory** command to list all hosts:

```
ansible-inventory --list -y
```

This command should display the dynamic inventory generated from AWS, confirming that Ansible can read and interpret it correctly.

Test the Dynamic Inventory

Create a new playbook file to test the dynamic inventory setup:

```
nano ~/GitforGits/playbooks/test_aws_inventory.yml
```

Copy the following:

```
---
- name: Test AWS Dynamic Inventory
  hosts: all
  tasks:
    - name: Ping all hosts
      ping:
```

Execute the playbook to verify that Ansible can connect to all hosts listed in the dynamic inventory:

```
ansible-playbook
~/GitforGits/playbooks/test_aws_inventory.yml
```

Advanced Configuration

You can extend and customize your dynamic inventory setup based on your needs. Following are some additional configurations you might consider:

- **Filter Instances by Tags:** Add filters to include or exclude instances based on specific tags.
- **Combine Inventories:** Combine AWS inventory with other cloud providers or static inventories.
- **Use Environment Variables:** Store sensitive information like AWS keys in environment variables for better security.

Example of Advanced Configuration

Update your **aws_ec2.yml** file to include additional filters or tags:

```
plugin: aws_ec2
```

```yaml
regions:
  - us-east-1
  - us-west-2
filters:
  instance-state-name: running
  tag:Environment: production
keyed_groups:
  - key: tags.Role
    prefix: role
hostnames:
  - tag:Name
compose:
  ansible_host: public_ip_address
```

Automate Updates with Cron Jobs

You can automate the update of your dynamic inventory by running the **ansible-inventory** command at regular intervals using a cron job. This ensures your inventory stays up-to-date without manual intervention.

Create a cron job:

```
crontab -e
```

Add the following line to run the inventory update every hour:

```
0 * * * * ansible-inventory --list -y >
/path/to/your/ansible/directory/inventory/aws_ec2_invento
ry.json
```

By following these steps, you have successfully set up and used a dynamic inventory for AWS EC2 instances. This approach ensures that your inventory is always current, making it ideal for dynamic and large-scale environments. Dynamic inventories provide the automation and scalability needed to efficiently manage cloud resources.

Recipe #8: Troubleshooting Inventory Issues

Managing inventories can sometimes lead to various issues, especially when dealing with dynamic and complex environments. Common inventory issues include connection problems, incorrect inventory paths, misconfigured variables, outdated inventory data, and authentication failures. This recipe will demonstrate in identifying and resolving these common issues to ensure your Ansible inventories function smoothly.

Common Inventory Issues

- **Connection Problems:** Inability to connect to hosts due to incorrect SSH keys, network issues, or wrong hostnames/IP addresses.
- **Incorrect Inventory Paths:** Ansible cannot find the inventory file due to incorrect paths specified in **`ansible.cfg`**.
- **Misconfigured Variables:** Errors in variable definitions or variable files can cause playbooks to fail.
- **Outdated Inventory Data:** Static inventories becoming outdated, leading to inconsistencies.
- **Authentication Failures:** Incorrect or missing credentials for cloud providers or other external systems.
- **Plugin Issues:** Misconfiguration or missing dependencies for inventory plugins.

In this recipe, we will provide troubleshooting steps to resolve common inventory issues, ensuring smooth and reliable inventory management.

Verify Inventory File Paths

Ensure that the inventory file paths specified in your **ansible.cfg** file are correct. Open the configuration file:

```
nano ~/GitforGits/ansible.cfg
```

Verify the inventory path:

```
[defaults]

inventory = inventory/aws_ec2/aws_ec2.yml
```

Ensure the path is correct and the file exists.

Test SSH Connectivity

Check SSH connectivity to your hosts manually to ensure there are no issues with SSH keys or network configurations:

```
ssh user@web1.gitforgits.com
```

If there are issues, verify the SSH keys and network settings.

Validate Dynamic Inventory Configuration

For dynamic inventories, validate the configuration file. Use the **ansible-inventory** command to check for errors:

```
ansible-inventory --list -y
```

This command will display any syntax or configuration errors in the dynamic inventory file.

Debug Variable Issues

If there are issues with variables, use the **debug** module in your playbooks to print variable values and check for misconfigurations:

```
---

- name: Debug Variables

  hosts: all

  tasks:
```

```
- name: Print variable values
  debug:
    var: your_variable
```

Run the playbook to see the output and identify any incorrect variable values.

Update Outdated Static Inventories

Static inventories can become outdated as infrastructure changes. Regularly update the inventory file to reflect the current state of your environment. Use a version control system like Git to track changes and ensure consistency.

Resolve Authentication Failures

For cloud-based dynamic inventories, ensure that your credentials are correctly configured. Check your AWS credentials file:

```
nano ~/.aws/credentials
```

Ensure the correct access keys are specified. For other cloud providers, verify the respective credential configurations.

Verify Plugin Dependencies

Ensure all required dependencies for inventory plugins are installed. For AWS, you need **boto3** and **botocore**. For other plugins, refer to their documentation for required packages.

Check for Plugin-Specific Issues

For inventory plugins, check the configuration and any specific settings required by the plugin. Ensure the configuration file includes all necessary fields and correct values.

Use Verbose Mode for Detailed Output

Use verbose mode to get detailed output from Ansible commands, which can help identify the root cause of issues. Run your playbooks with increased verbosity:

```
ansible-playbook playbook.yml -vvv
```

This provides detailed logs and error messages that can help in troubleshooting.

Use Ansible Documentation and Community Support

Refer to the Ansible documentation and community forums for solutions to common issues. The Ansible community is active, and many common problems have been addressed by other users.

By following these steps, you can effectively troubleshoot and resolve common inventory issues. Ensuring that your inventories are correctly configured and up-to-date is crucial for smooth and reliable automation workflows. This approach helps maintain the integrity of your infrastructure management and prevents disruptions caused by inventory-related problems.

Summary

Here in this chapter, you learned the basics of Ansible inventory management, beginning with static inventory setup, which allowed you to manually list and group hosts in a simple way. Following this, you studied the development of dynamic inventories, which automatically generated and updated host lists from external data sources, such as cloud providers. This technique was especially advantageous in dynamic environments, as it guaranteed that inventories were consistently up-to-date.

Additionally, you developed expertise regarding inventory plugins, which enabled the seamless integration of a variety of external systems and services, thereby further automating the inventory management process. We spoke about how to group hosts in inventories, which could help you manage your infrastructure better by classifying hosts according to their roles or some other logical criterion. The technique facilitated the management of large-scale environments and guaranteed consistent configurations across groups.

Another significant topic was the use of host and group variables, which enabled the creation of personalized configurations for particular hosts or groups. Along with learning how to manage inventory files, you also learned how to use Git, which offers features like version control, collaboration, and backup. Because of this, we could keep tabs on all of the changes and roll back to earlier versions with ease.

We also went over how to use AWS to connect to cloud instances with dynamic inventories so you can manage your cloud resources efficiently with plugins. In the end, we covered how to troubleshoot inventory issues, which includes common problems like connection problems, wrong inventory paths, misconfigured variables, outdated data, authentication failures, and plugin issues, among others.

Ultimately, this chapter has provided you with the necessary skills to effectively manage Ansible inventories, thus assuring that your automation tasks are executed seamlessly across all managed hosts, irrespective of the complexity or size of your environment.

Knowledge Exercise

Question 1: What is the primary function of an inventory in Ansible?
A) To store playbooks
B) To define and group the hosts managed by Ansible
C) To configure Ansible plugins
D) To manage Ansible roles

Answer:
B) To define and group the hosts managed by Ansible

An inventory in Ansible lists the managed nodes and groups them into categories, allowing targeted execution of playbooks.

Question 2: Which of the following is a key benefit of using static inventories?
A) Automatic updates from cloud providers
B) Simple and straightforward host management
C) Integration with external systems
D) Dynamic grouping of hosts

Answer:
B) Simple and straightforward host management

Static inventories are simple text files where hosts and groups are listed manually, making them straightforward to manage.

Question 3: Which command is used to verify the dynamic inventory setup in Ansible?
A) **ansible-playbook**
B) **ansible-inventory**
C) **ansible-config**
D) **ansible-debug**

Answer:
B) **ansible-inventory**

The **ansible-inventory** command lists all hosts and verifies the dynamic inventory setup.

Question 4: What file format is typically used to define inventory files in Ansible?
A) JSON
B) XML
C) INI
D) CSV

Answer:
C) INI

Inventory files in Ansible are typically defined in the INI format, though YAML and JSON formats can also be used.

Question 5: How are group variables defined in an Ansible inventory?
A) In the playbook

B) In the **ansible.cfg** file
C) Under the **[group:vars]** section in the inventory file
D) In the environment variables

Answer:
C) Under the **[group:vars]** section in the inventory file

Group variables are defined under the **[group:vars]** section in the inventory file, allowing customization for specific groups.

Question 6: Which package needs to be installed to use AWS EC2 as a dynamic inventory source?
A) **boto3**
B) **azure**
C) **requests**
D) **paramiko**

Answer:
A) **boto3**

The **boto3** package is required to interact with AWS services and use AWS EC2 as a dynamic inventory source.

Question 7: What is the primary purpose of using inventory plugins in Ansible?
A) To define playbooks
B) To dynamically generate inventory from external sources
C) To manage SSH keys
D) To execute ad-hoc commands

Answer:
B) To dynamically generate inventory from external sources

Inventory plugins dynamically generate inventory from various external sources, ensuring the inventory is always current.

Question 8: Which section in the **ansible.cfg** file specifies the path to the inventory file?
A) **[plugins]**
B) **[inventory]**
C) **[defaults]**
D) **[vars]**

Answer:
C) **[defaults]**

The **[defaults]** section in the **ansible.cfg** file specifies the path to the inventory file.

Question 9: What does the **plugin** keyword specify in a dynamic inventory configuration file?
A) The inventory file format
B) The external source type

C) The location of the playbooks
D) The Ansible version

Answer:
B) The external source type

The **plugin** keyword in a dynamic inventory configuration file specifies the type of external source, such as **aws_ec2** for AWS EC2.

Question 10: Which command allows you to manually test SSH connectivity to a host listed in the inventory?
A) **ansible-ssh**
B) **ansible-ping**
C) **ssh**
D) **connect**

Answer:
C) **ssh**

The **ssh** command allows you to manually test SSH connectivity to a host listed in the inventory.

Question 11: What is a common reason for authentication failures when using dynamic inventories with cloud providers?
A) Incorrect inventory file format
B) Misconfigured or missing credentials
C) Incorrect playbook syntax
D) Unsupported Ansible version

Answer:
B) Misconfigured or missing credentials

Authentication failures often occur due to misconfigured or missing credentials required to interact with the cloud provider.

Question 12: How can you organize hosts based on their roles in an Ansible inventory file?
A) By using tags
B) By using variables
C) By grouping them under role-specific sections
D) By using environment variables

Answer:
C) By grouping them under role-specific sections

Hosts can be organized based on their roles by grouping them under role-specific sections in the inventory file, such as **[webservers]** or **[databases]**.

Question 13: Which Ansible command provides detailed output and error messages useful for troubleshooting?

A) **ansible-debug**
B) **ansible-playbook -vvv**
C) **ansible-inventory --check**
D) **ansible-config**

Answer:
B) **ansible-playbook -vvv**

Using **ansible-playbook -vvv** provides detailed output and error messages, which are useful for troubleshooting.

Question 14: What is the purpose of the **filters** keyword in a dynamic inventory configuration for AWS EC2?
A) To specify the Ansible version
B) To define playbook paths
C) To filter EC2 instances based on specific criteria
D) To configure SSH keys

Answer:
C) To filter EC2 instances based on specific criteria

The **filters** keyword in a dynamic inventory configuration for AWS EC2 is used to filter instances based on criteria such as instance state or tags.

Question 15: Which file typically stores AWS credentials for dynamic inventory configuration in Ansible?
A) **~/.aws/credentials**
B) **/etc/ansible/credentials**
C) **~/.ansible/aws_credentials**
D) **/var/lib/ansible/credentials**

Answer:
A) **~/.aws/credentials**

AWS credentials are typically stored in the **~/.aws/credentials** file for dynamic inventory configuration in Ansible.

Question 16: How can you automate the update of a dynamic inventory file?
A) By using a cron job
B) By manually editing the inventory file
C) By running ad-hoc commands
D) By updating the **ansible.cfg** file

Answer:
A) By using a cron job

You can automate the update of a dynamic inventory file by scheduling the **ansible-inventory** command to run at regular intervals using a cron job.

Question 17: What is a common cause of connection problems when using Ansible inventories?
A) Incorrect playbook syntax
B) Incorrect SSH keys or network configurations
C) Misconfigured variables
D) Outdated Ansible version

Answer:
B) Incorrect SSH keys or network configurations

Connection problems often arise due to incorrect SSH keys or network configurations, preventing Ansible from connecting to the hosts.

Question 18: Which section of the **ansible.cfg** file allows you to specify multiple inventory files?
A) **[inventory]**
B) **[defaults]**
C) **[vars]**
D) **[plugins]**

Answer:
B) **[defaults]**

The **[defaults]** section of the **ansible.cfg** file allows you to specify multiple inventory files.

Question 19: How are host variables typically defined in Ansible inventories?
A) In the **ansible.cfg** file
B) Under the **[host_vars]** directory
C) In the playbook
D) In the environment variables

Answer:
B) Under the **[host_vars]** directory

Host variables are typically defined under the **[host_vars]** directory, allowing customization for specific hosts.

Question 20: Which command can you use to add files to a Git repository managing your Ansible inventory?
A) **git add**
B) **git commit**
C) **git push**
D) **git status**

Answer:
A) **git add**

The **git add** command stages changes, adding files to the Git repository managing your Ansible inventory.

CHAPTER 4: ADVANCED PLAYBOOK TECHNIQUES

Introduction

Everything you need to know about Ansible environments, playbooks, and inventory management has been covered so far. You now know how to organize hosts, manage variables, create static and dynamic inventories, and integrate with cloud providers. You have been equipped to manage basic and intermediate automation tasks with Ansible as a result of these specific skills.

Here, in this chapter, you will learn advanced playbook techniques to boost your automation skills. To facilitate the development of reusable and modular code, you will initially learn the skill to apply roles to effectively organize playbooks. Subsequently, you will learn how to develop and implement customized modules, which will enhance Ansible's capabilities to accommodate particular needs. We will go over how to implement error handling in playbooks so that automation scripts are strong and dependable.

Another critical topic is the encryption of critical information within your playbooks using Ansible Vault to secure sensitive data. You will also acquire the ability to utilize Ansible Galaxy to access a vast repository of community-contributed roles and modules, thereby utilizing reusable content. You can generate dynamic configurations by creating playbook templates with Jinja2. Regardless of the number of times a playbook is executed, implementing idempotency can ensure consistent results. Finally, you can learn how to speed up and improve the efficiency of your automation processes by optimizing the performance of your playbooks.

Upon completion of this chapter, you will have picked up the ability to perform sophisticated techniques that will substantially enhance the maintainability and efficacy of your Ansible playbooks.

Recipe #1: Using Roles to Organize Playbooks

Roles are a powerful way to organize playbooks into reusable, modular components. They enable you to encapsulate tasks, variables, handlers, and other playbook elements, making your automation code more maintainable and scalable. Roles can be reused across multiple playbooks and projects, promoting consistency and reducing duplication.

Types of Roles

1. **Custom Roles:** Created specifically for your needs, custom roles encapsulate tasks, variables, and configurations tailored to your infrastructure and application requirements.
2. **Community Roles:** Available on Ansible Galaxy, these roles are shared by the community and can be used to implement common configurations and tasks.
3. **Organizational Roles:** Developed and maintained within an organization, these roles follow internal standards and practices, ensuring consistency across different teams and projects.

With this recipe, you will understand to use roles to organize playbooks, creating a modular and reusable structure for your automation code.

Create Role Directory Structure

Roles follow a specific directory structure. Create a new role using the **ansible-galaxy** command:

```
cd ~/GitforGits

ansible-galaxy init roles/webserver
```

This command creates the following directory structure:

```
roles/webserver/

├── defaults

│   └── main.yml

├── files

├── handlers

│   └── main.yml

├── meta

│   └── main.yml

├── tasks

│   └── main.yml

├── templates

├── tests

│   ├── inventory

│   └── test.yml
```

```
└── vars

    └── main.yml
```

Define Role Tasks

Open the **tasks/main.yml** file in your role and define the tasks for the webserver role. If you've previously configured a webserver, refer back to those steps rather than repeating them here.

```
nano roles/webserver/tasks/main.yml
```

Add the following script to reference tasks for the webserver:

```
---

# Refer to previous steps for Nginx installation and configuration.

- name: Ensure Nginx is installed and configured

  include_role:

    name: webserver_install
```

Define Handlers

Open the **handlers/main.yml** file and define the handler to restart Nginx:

```
nano roles/webserver/handlers/main.yml
```

Copy the following:

```
---

- name: Restart Nginx

  service:

    name: nginx
```

```
    state: restarted
```

Define Variables

Open the **defaults/main.yml** file and define default variables for the role:

```
nano roles/webserver/defaults/main.yml
```

Copy the following:

```
---

nginx_port: 80
```

Create Templates

Place any configuration templates in the **templates** directory. Create an Nginx configuration template:

```
nano roles/webserver/templates/nginx.conf.j2
```

Copy the following:

```
server {

    listen {{ nginx_port }};

    server_name localhost;


    location / {

        root /var/www/html;

        index index.html index.htm;

    }
```

```
}
```

Create a playbook to use the webserver role:

```
nano playbooks/deploy_webserver.yml
```

Copy the following:

```
---

- name: Deploy Webserver

  hosts: webservers

  roles:

    - webserver
```

Define Inventory

Ensure your inventory file includes the **webservers** group:

```
nano inventory/hosts
```

Copy the following:

```
[webservers]

web1.gitforgits.com

web2.gitforgits.com
```

Execute the playbook and you will see that you have successfully created and used a role to organize your playbooks. Roles promote modularity, reusability, and maintainability, making it easier to manage complex automation tasks.

Recipe #2: Creating and using Custom

Modules

Custom modules extend its functionality by allowing you to write your own modules to perform specific tasks that are not covered by built-in modules. This can be particularly useful for integrating with proprietary systems or implementing specialized operations.

Our goal in this recipe is to create and use custom modules, enhancing the flexibility and power of your automation scripts.

Create Custom Module Script

Custom modules are typically written in Python. Create a directory for your custom modules and a new Python script for your custom module:

```
mkdir -p ~/GitforGits/library

nano ~/GitforGits/library/my_custom_module.py
```

Add the given below script to the Python script:

```
#!/usr/bin/python


from ansible.module_utils.basic import AnsibleModule


def run_module():
    module_args = dict(
        name=dict(type='str', required=True)
    )


    result = dict(
        changed=False,
```

```
        original_message='',
        message=''
    )
    module = AnsibleModule(
        argument_spec=module_args,
        supports_check_mode=True
    )

    name = module.params['name']

    result['original_message'] = name
    result['message'] = f'Hello, {name}!'

    if module.check_mode:
        module.exit_json(**result)

    result['changed'] = True
    module.exit_json(**result)

def main():
    run_module()
```

```
if __name__ == '__main__':
    main()
```

This simple custom module takes a **name** parameter and returns a greeting message. Now, ensure the custom module script is executable:

```
chmod +x ~/GitforGits/library/my_custom_module.py
```

Use Custom Module

Create a new playbook to use the custom module:

```
nano ~/GitforGits/playbooks/use_custom_module.yml
```

Add the script as given below:

```
---
- name: Use Custom Module
  hosts: localhost
  tasks:
    - name: Greet with custom module
      my_custom_module:
        name: Ansible
      register: result

    - name: Print result
      debug:
```

```
        var: result.message
```

Define Inventory

Ensure your inventory file includes the **localhost** group:

```
nano inventory/hosts

[localhost]

127.0.0.1
```

After running the playbook, verify it has printed the greeting message. With these steps, you have successfully created and used a custom module. Custom modules allow you to extend Ansible's functionality to meet specific needs, providing greater flexibility and power in your automation scripts.

Recipe #3: Implementing Error Handling in Playbooks

Implementing error handling in Ansible playbooks is essential to ensure robust and reliable automation. Proper error handling helps you manage failures gracefully, provides meaningful feedback, and allows you to take corrective actions.

In this recipe, you will learn to implement error handling in Ansible playbooks, ensuring that automation tasks are resilient and provide useful error information.

'failed_when' Directive

The **failed_when** directive allows you to specify conditions under which a task is considered failed. This can be useful for tasks where the default failure conditions are not sufficient.

Create a new playbook file:

```
nano ~/GitforGits/playbooks/error_handling.yml
```

Add the script as given below:

```
---
```

```
- name: Demonstrate Error Handling
  hosts: localhost
  tasks:
    - name: Check free disk space
      command: df -h /
      register: disk_space

    - name: Fail if free space is less than 10%
      debug:
        msg: "Free space is sufficient: {{
disk_space.stdout }}"
      failed_when: "'10%' in disk_space.stdout"
```

In the above sample code, the task will fail if the free disk space is less than 10%.

'ignore_errors' Directive

The **ignore_errors** directive allows a playbook to continue execution even if a task fails. This can be useful for non-critical tasks where you want the playbook to proceed regardless of the outcome.

Add the following task to the same playbook:

```
   - name: Attempt to create a directory
      command: mkdir /already_exists
      ignore_errors: yes

    - name: Notify of failure
```

```
      debug:

         msg: "Previous task failed, but playbook
continues."
```

In the above sample code, the playbook will continue even if the directory creation fails.

'rescue' and 'always' Blocks

The **block**, **rescue**, and **always** directives allow for more advanced error handling by grouping tasks and specifying actions to take on failure.

Add the following block to the playbook:

```
    - name: Error Handling with Block

      block:

        - name: Attempt to download a file

          get_url:

            url: http://gitforgits.com/non_existent_file

            dest: /tmp/non_existent_file


        - name: Notify of download success

          debug:

            msg: "File downloaded successfully."


      rescue:

        - name: Handle download failure

          debug:
```

```
          msg: "Download failed. Proceeding with
alternative actions."

      always:
        - name: Cleanup actions
          file:
            path: /tmp/non_existent_file
            state: absent
```

In the above sample code, if the file download fails, the tasks in the **rescue** block will execute, and the **always** block will execute regardless of the success or failure of the previous tasks.

After running the playbook, check the output for the specified error handling messages and actions. If all goes good, then you can say that you have successfully implemented error handling and can recover gracefully from failures.

Recipe #4: Using Ansible Vault for Securing Sensitive Data

Introduction to Ansible Vault

Ansible Vault is a feature that allows you to keep sensitive data such as passwords or keys in encrypted files, rather than as plaintext in your playbooks or roles. Ansible Vault is designed to encrypt and decrypt files within your Ansible projects. This allows you to store sensitive information securely and use it within your playbooks without exposing it to unauthorized access. Vault can encrypt entire files or specific variables within a file, providing flexibility in how you secure your data.

Following are the key characteristics of Vault:

1. **Encryption and Decryption:** Encrypts files using AES256 encryption, and decrypts them for use during playbook execution.
2. **Password Protection:** Files encrypted with Vault require a password to decrypt, adding a layer of security.

3. **File and Variable Encryption:** Encrypt entire files or specific variables, allowing granular control over what data is encrypted.
4. **Integration with Playbooks:** Easily integrates with Ansible playbooks, allowing seamless use of encrypted data during playbook runs.

In this recipe, you will learn to use Ansible Vault to secure sensitive data, including creating, editing, and using encrypted files within playbooks.

Install Ansible Vault

Ansible Vault is included with Ansible by default. Ensure you have Ansible installed:

```
ansible --version
```

Create Encrypted File

Use the **ansible-vault create** command to create a new encrypted file:

```
cd ~/GitforGits

ansible-vault create secrets.yml
```

You will be prompted to enter a password. This password will be used to encrypt and decrypt the file. After entering the password, a text editor will open. Add the following code snippet:

```
db_password: "supersecretpassword"
```

Save and close the file.

Manage Encrypted Files

To view the contents of an encrypted file, use the **ansible-vault view** command:

```
ansible-vault view secrets.yml
```

To edit the contents of an encrypted file, use the **ansible-vault edit** command:

```
ansible-vault edit secrets.yml
```

You can also encrypt an existing plaintext file using the **ansible-vault encrypt** command:

```
ansible-vault encrypt inventory/hosts
```

You will be prompted to enter a password to encrypt the file. Similarly, to decrypt an encrypted file and convert it back to plaintext, use the **ansible-vault decrypt** command:

```
ansible-vault decrypt secrets.yml
```

Using Encrypted Files in Playbooks

To use encrypted variables in a playbook, include the encrypted file using the **vars_files** directive:

```
nano ~/GitforGits/playbooks/use_vault.yml
```

Add the following code snippet:

```
---

- name: Use Ansible Vault

  hosts: localhost

  vars_files:

    - ../secrets.yml

  tasks:

    - name: Print the decrypted password

      debug:

        msg: "The database password is {{ db_password }}"
```

Execute the playbook using the **ansible-playbook** command. You will be prompted to enter the vault password to decrypt the file:

```
ansible-playbook ~/GitforGits/playbooks/use_vault.yml --
ask-vault-pass
```

Automate Vault Password Handling

To avoid being prompted for the password every time, you can use a password file. Create a file to store the vault password:

```
echo 'your_vault_password' > ~/GitforGits/.vault_pass.txt
```

Ensure this file has restricted permissions:

```
chmod 600 ~/GitforGits/.vault_pass.txt
```

Modify the playbook command to use the password file:

```
ansible-playbook ~/GitforGits/playbooks/use_vault.yml --
vault-password-file ~/GitforGits/.vault_pass.txt
```

By following these steps, you have successfully used Ansible Vault to secure sensitive data.

Recipe #5: Leveraging Ansible Galaxy for Reusable Content

Introduction to Ansible Galaxy

Ansible Galaxy is a hub for finding, sharing, and reusing Ansible roles. It allows you to leverage pre-built roles created by the Ansible community to speed up your automation projects. Galaxy hosts a wide variety of roles for different purposes, from installing and configuring software to managing cloud resources and infrastructure.

Following are the key features of Galaxy:

- **Role Repository:** A central repository of Ansible roles contributed by the community.
- **Ease of Use:** Simple commands to install and manage roles from Galaxy.
- **Reusability:** Reuse existing roles to save time and avoid reinventing the wheel.
- **Community Contributions:** Access to a vast library of roles contributed by Ansible users worldwide.

Our goal in this recipe is to leverage Ansible Galaxy for reusable content by installing and using community roles in your playbooks.

Browse and Search for Roles

Ensure you have the Ansible Galaxy CLI installed. It is included with Ansible by default:

```
ansible-galaxy --version
```

Visit the Ansible Galaxy website (https://galaxy.ansible.com/) to browse and search for roles. Use the search functionality to find roles that match your needs.

Install Role from Ansible Galaxy

Use the **ansible-galaxy install** command to install a role. For example, to install a role for setting up Nginx, you might find a popular role like **geerlingguy.nginx**:

```
ansible-galaxy install geerlingguy.nginx
```

This command downloads the role and places it in the **roles/** directory within your Ansible project.

Use Role in Playbook

Create a new playbook to use the installed role:

```
nano ~/GitforGits/playbooks/use_galaxy_role.yml
```

Add the given below script to use the **geerlingguy.nginx** role:

```
---

- name: Use Ansible Galaxy Role

  hosts: webservers

  roles:

    - geerlingguy.nginx
```

Open your inventory file and add the given below script if not already present:

```
[webservers]
```

```
web1.gitforgits.com
web2.gitforgits.com
```

Customize Role Variables

Many roles from Ansible Galaxy come with configurable variables. Customize these variables to fit your needs. Open the **group_vars/webservers.yml** file (create it if it doesn't exist):

```
nano ~/GitforGits/inventory/group_vars/webservers.yml
```

Add the following script to customize the Nginx role variables:

```
nginx_vhosts:
  - server_name: "gitforgits.com"
    root: "/var/www/gitforgits.com"
  - server_name: "test.com"
    root: "/var/www/test.com"
```

Re-run the playbook to apply the customized variables:

```
ansible-playbook
~/GitforGits/playbooks/use_galaxy_role.yml
```

Many roles have dependencies on other roles. These dependencies are specified in the role's metadata file (**meta/main.yml**). Ansible Galaxy automatically installs these dependencies when you install a role. Using roles from Ansible Galaxy saves time, ensures best practices, and allows you to enhance your ability to implement robust and efficient automation solutions.

Recipe #6: Creating Playbook Templates with Jinja2

Jinja2 Overview

Jinja2 is a powerful templating engine for Python, widely used for creating dynamic and flexible templates. Jinja2 allows you to embed variables, use control structures like loops and conditionals, and include macros to generate dynamic content. It is the default templating engine used by Ansible for creating configuration files, scripts, and other text-based outputs. Followiing are the traits that makes Jinja2 a better templating engine:

- **Variable Substitution:** Embed variables in templates to create dynamic content.
- **Control Structures:** Use loops and conditionals to control the output based on variables and conditions.
- **Filters:** Apply filters to variables to modify their output.
- **Macros:** Reuse code snippets within templates for better maintainability.

By this recipe, you will understand to create and use playbook templates with Jinja2, enabling dynamic and flexible configuration management.

Create Jinja2 Template

Create a new directory for your templates if it doesn't exist:

```
mkdir -p ~/GitforGits/templates
```

Create a Jinja2 template file for Nginx configuration:

```
nano ~/GitforGits/templates/nginx.conf.j2
```

Add the given below script to the template file:

```
server {
    listen {{ nginx_port }};
    server_name {{ server_name }};

    location / {
        root {{ document_root }};
        index index.html index.htm;
```

```
    }
}
```

Define Variables

Create a new playbook file to use the Jinja2 template:

```
nano ~/GitforGits/playbooks/use_template.yml
```

Add the given below script to define the variables and apply the template:

```
---
- name: Use Jinja2 Template
  hosts: webservers
  vars:
    nginx_port: 80
    server_name: gitforgits.com
    document_root: /var/www/gitforgits.com
  tasks:
    - name: Deploy Nginx configuration from template
      template:
        src: ../templates/nginx.conf.j2
        dest: /etc/nginx/nginx.conf
      notify:
        - Restart Nginx
```

```
handlers:
  - name: Restart Nginx
    service:
      name: nginx
      state: restarted
```

After running the playbook, verify the Nginx configuration file has been created on the target hosts with the variables substituted:

```
ssh user@web1.gitforgits.com
cat /etc/nginx/nginx.conf
```

You should see the configuration file with the actual values substituted for **nginx_port**, **server_name**, and **document_root**.

Using Loops, Conditional and Filters

Jinja2 also supports advanced features such as loops, conditionals, and filters. Update the template file to include a loop for multiple server names:

```
nano ~/GitforGits/templates/nginx.conf.j2
```

Add the script as given below:

```
server {
    listen {{ nginx_port }};
    server_name {% for name in server_names %}{{ name }}
{% endfor %};

    location / {
```

```
        root {{ document_root }};
        index index.html index.htm;
    }
}
```

Update the playbook to define the **server_names** variable as a list:

```
nano ~/GitforGits/playbooks/use_template.yml
```

Modify the **vars** section:

```
vars:
  nginx_port: 80
  server_names:
    - gitforgits.com
    - www.gitforgits.com
  document_root: /var/www/gitforgits.com
```

Re-run the playbook to apply the updated template:

```
ansible-playbook ~/GitforGits/playbooks/use_template.yml
```

Verify Advanced Template

After running the playbook, verify the advanced template on the target hosts:

```
ssh user@web1.gitforgits.com
cat /etc/nginx/nginx.conf
```

The server names should now include both **gitforgits.com** and **www.gitforgits.com**.

So now, you have successfully created and used playbook templates with Jinja2 to create dynamic and flexible configurations.

Recipe #7: Implementing Idempotency in Playbooks

Concept of Idempotency

Idempotency refers to the property of playbooks and tasks to be run multiple times without changing the result beyond the initial application. In other words, running the same playbook multiple times should have the same effect as running it once. Idempotent tasks ensure that the system reaches and maintains a desired state without causing unintended changes or disruptions when rerun.

In this recipe, you will learn to implement idempotency in Ansible playbooks, ensuring that tasks can be safely rerun without causing unintended changes.

Implement Idempotency in a Playbook

Before we begin, review your playbooks to identify tasks that might not be idempotent. For example, tasks that create or modify files, install packages, or start services can be made idempotent by using the appropriate Ansible modules and conditions.

We will use the previously created playbook that sets up an Nginx web server (**deploy_webserver.yml**).

Installing Nginx

The **apt** module used for installing Nginx is already idempotent. It checks whether Nginx is installed and only installs it if necessary.

```
- name: Ensure Nginx is installed

  apt:

    name: nginx

    state: present
```

Deploying Nginx Configuration

Using the **template** module is idempotent as it only updates the file if the content changes.

```
- name: Deploy Nginx configuration from template
  template:
    src: ../templates/nginx.conf.j2
    dest: /etc/nginx/nginx.conf
  notify:
    - Restart Nginx
```

Starting Nginx Service

The **service** module ensures that the service is running and restarts it only if necessary.

```
- name: Ensure Nginx is running
  service:
    name: nginx
    state: started
```

Update Playbook

Create or update the playbook to ensure it implements idempotency. Following is the complete playbook:

```
---
- name: Deploy Webserver
  hosts: webservers
  become: yes
  tasks:
```

```
  - name: Ensure Nginx is installed
    apt:
      name: nginx
      state: present

  - name: Deploy Nginx configuration from template
    template:
      src: ../templates/nginx.conf.j2
      dest: /etc/nginx/nginx.conf
    notify:
      - Restart Nginx

  - name: Ensure Nginx is running
    service:
      name: nginx
      state: started

handlers:
  - name: Restart Nginx
    service:
      name: nginx
```

```
        state: restarted
```

Before running the playbook, ensure the inventory file includes the **webservers** group:

```
ansible-playbook
~/GitforGits/playbooks/deploy_webserver.yml
```

Verify Idempotency

Run the playbook multiple times to ensure it maintains idempotency. The output should indicate that no changes were made if the system is already in the desired state:

```
ansible-playbook
~/GitforGits/playbooks/deploy_webserver.yml
```

With this, you have successfully implemented idempotency in an Ansible playbook.

Recipe #8: Optimizing Playbook Performance

Introduction to Playbook Performance Optimization

The optimization of playbook performance involves techniques and best practices that reduce execution time, minimize resource usage, and improve the efficiency of your automation tasks. The efficient playbooks ensure faster deployments and updates, making your automation processes more scalable and reliable.

In this recipe, you will learn to enhance and improve the performance of previously implemented playbooks by using various optimization techniques.

Enable Fact Caching

Fact caching stores gathered facts about hosts, reducing the need to gather them every time a playbook runs. This can significantly reduce execution time for playbooks that run frequently.

Open your **ansible.cfg** file:

```
nano ~/GitforGits/ansible.cfg
```

Add the following configuration to enable fact caching using JSON file backend:

```
[defaults]

fact_caching = jsonfile

fact_caching_connection = /tmp/ansible_cache

fact_caching_timeout = 86400
```

'async' and 'poll' for Long-Running Tasks

For tasks that take a long time to complete, use **async** and **poll** to run them asynchronously, allowing other tasks to execute concurrently. To do this, update the playbook to install Nginx asynchronously:

```
- name: Ensure Nginx is installed

  apt:

    name: nginx

    state: present

  async: 300

  poll: 0

  register: nginx_install


- name: Wait for Nginx installation to complete

  async_status:

    jid: "{{ nginx_install.ansible_job_id }}"

  register: nginx_install_status

  until: nginx_install_status.finished

  retries: 30
```

```
  delay: 10
```

Limit Parallelism with 'forks'

Increase the number of parallel processes (forks) to run more tasks simultaneously. This can speed up playbook execution in environments with many hosts. For this, open your **ansible.cfg** file, add the following configuration to increase the number of forks:

```
nano ~/GitforGits/ansible.cfg

[defaults]

forks = 10
```

Reduce SSH Connection Overhead

Reuse SSH connections to reduce the overhead of establishing new connections for each task. Enable SSH connection reuse in your **ansible.cfg** file:

```
[ssh_connection]

retries = 3

pipelining = True

control_path = %(directory)s/%%h-%%r
```

'delegate_to' for Centralized Operations

Delegate tasks that don't need to run on each host to a central node to reduce redundant operations. For example, updating DNS records can be done from a single node.

```
- name: Update DNS records

  command: /usr/bin/update-dns

  delegate_to: localhost
```

Optimize Task Execution

Use conditionals to skip tasks that don't need to be run. This avoids unnecessary operations and speeds up playbook execution.

```
- name: Ensure Nginx is installed

  apt:

    name: nginx

    state: present

  when: ansible_distribution == 'Ubuntu'
```

'block' for Grouping Tasks

Group related tasks using **block** to manage dependencies and error handling more efficiently.

```
- block:

    - name: Install dependencies

      apt:

        name: "{{ item }}"

        state: present

      loop:

        - libpcre3

        - libpcre3-dev

        - zlib1g-dev


    - name: Compile and install Nginx

      command: ./configure && make && make install
```

```
  when: ansible_os_family == 'Debian'
```

Next, you cache results of expensive operations and reuse them to avoid redundant processing.

```
- name: Check if Nginx is installed
  command: dpkg -l nginx
  register: nginx_installed
  changed_when: false


- name: Install Nginx if not installed
  apt:
    name: nginx
    state: present
  when: nginx_installed.rc != 0
```

Using the appropriate Ansible modules for specific tasks can be more efficient than using generic modules like **command** or **shell**. For example, use **apt** for package management instead of **command**.

Monitor Performance with Callback Plugins

Use callback plugins to monitor playbook performance and identify bottlenecks. The **profile_tasks** plugin can provide detailed timing information.

Open your **ansible.cfg** file:

```
nano ~/GitforGits/ansible.cfg
```

Add the following configuration to enable the **profile_tasks** plugin:

```
[defaults]
```

```
callback_whitelist = profile_tasks
```

Execute the optimized playbook using the **ansible-playbook** command:

```
ansible-playbook
~/GitforGits/playbooks/deploy_webserver.yml
```

By following these steps, you have optimized the performance of your Ansible playbooks.

Summary

Here in this chapter, we covered advanced playbook techniques, started with utilizing roles to organize playbooks and then looked at a variety of roles, such as custom, community, and organizational roles, and acquired the skills necessary to establish and execute them. After that, you learned building and utilizing custom modules to enhance Ansible's capabilities for specific tasks. In addition, you made use of directives such as failed_when, ignore_errors, and block to handle errors in playbooks, allowing for reliable execution and graceful failure management.

You learned how to secure sensitive data using Ansible Vault, which included creating, editing, encrypting, and decrypting files to safeguard confidential information within playbooks. Reusing community-contributed roles through Ansible Galaxy ensures best practices and saves time. Using variables, loops, conditionals, and filters, you generated dynamic configurations in Jinja2 to create playbook templates.

By incorporating idempotency into playbooks, we made sure that tasks could be reran without modifying the system in any way, shape, or form. You reviewed and updated tasks to ensure that they were idempotent, utilizing the appropriate modules and conditions. Lastly, you enhanced the performance of the playbook by enabling fact caching, utilizing async and poll for long-running tasks, increasing parallelism with forks, reusing SSH connections, delegating tasks, using conditionals, grouping tasks with blocks, caching results, using specific modules, and monitoring performance with callback plugins.

Taken together, the skills you learned in this chapter will help you manage complicated automation tasks better by allowing you to build Ansible playbooks that are efficient, dependable, and secure. These sophisticated abilities have enhanced the scalability, maintainability, and resilience of your automation processes.

Knowledge Exercise

Question 1: What is the primary purpose of using roles in Ansible?

A) To organize tasks within a playbook
B) To store inventory files
C) To define playbook variables
D) To create reusable and modular playbook components

Answer:
D) To create reusable and modular playbook components

Roles in Ansible are used to organize playbooks into reusable, modular components, promoting maintainability and consistency across different projects.

Question 2: Which command is used to create a new role in Ansible?
A) **ansible-role create**
B) **ansible-role init**
C) **ansible-galaxy create**
D) **ansible-galaxy init**

Answer:
D) **ansible-galaxy init**

The **ansible-galaxy init** command is used to create a new role with the standard directory structure.

Question 3: In the context of custom modules, what is the primary purpose of the **AnsibleModule** class?
A) To define inventory variables
B) To handle encryption and decryption of data
C) To manage arguments and results for custom modules
D) To execute playbooks asynchronously

Answer:
C) To manage arguments and results for custom modules

The **AnsibleModule** class in custom modules manages arguments, validates input, and handles results, ensuring proper communication between the module and Ansible.

Question 4: What directive is used to handle errors in Ansible playbooks by continuing execution even if a task fails?
A) **failed_when**
B) **ignore_errors**
C) **rescue**

D) **always**

Answer:
B) **ignore_errors**

The **ignore_errors** directive allows a playbook to continue execution even if a task fails.

Question 5: Which Ansible feature is used to encrypt sensitive data within playbooks?
A) Ansible Galaxy
B) Ansible Vault
C) Ansible Role
D) Ansible Template

Answer:
B) Ansible Vault

Ansible Vault is used to encrypt sensitive data within playbooks, ensuring secure storage and usage of confidential information.

Question 6: How do you install a role from Ansible Galaxy?
A) **ansible-galaxy install role_name**
B) **ansible-role install role_name**
C) **ansible-vault install role_name**
D) **ansible-galaxy create role_name**

Answer:
A) **ansible-galaxy install role_name**

The **ansible-galaxy install role_name** command installs a role from Ansible Galaxy, downloading it to the local roles directory.

Question 7: What is Jinja2 primarily used for in Ansible?
A) Encrypting playbooks
B) Creating dynamic templates
C) Defining inventory files
D) Managing playbook variables

Answer:
B) Creating dynamic templates

Jinja2 is a powerful templating engine used in Ansible for creating dynamic templates, allowing for variable substitution, control structures, and reusable code snippets.

Question 8: Which of the following directives ensures a task is considered failed only if a specified condition is met?
A) **when**
B) **changed_when**
C) **failed_when**
D) **check_mode**

Answer:
C) **failed_when**

The **failed_when** directive specifies a condition under which a task is considered failed, allowing for custom failure criteria.

Question 9: In Ansible, how can you run a task asynchronously and check its status later?
A) Using **wait_for**
B) Using **async** and **poll**
C) Using **delegate_to**
D) Using **ignore_errors**

Answer:
B) Using **async** and **poll**

Using **async** and **poll** allows a task to run asynchronously, with the ability to check its status later, enabling concurrent task execution.

Question 10: Which configuration option in **ansible.cfg** is used to increase the number of parallel processes (forks)?
A) **fact_caching**
B) **async**
C) **forks**
D) **retries**

Answer:
C) **forks**

The **forks** configuration option in **ansible.cfg** increases the number of parallel processes, allowing more tasks to run simultaneously.

Question 11: What is the benefit of using the **template** module in Ansible playbooks?

A) To encrypt playbooks
B) To create and manage inventory files
C) To deploy dynamic configuration files
D) To execute playbooks asynchronously

Answer:
C) To deploy dynamic configuration files

The **template** module is used to deploy dynamic configuration files using Jinja2 templates, allowing for variable substitution and control structures.

Question 12: How does the **block** directive help in managing tasks in Ansible playbooks?
A) By defining inventory variables
B) By grouping related tasks and managing error handling
C) By storing sensitive data securely
D) By running tasks in parallel

Answer:
B) By grouping related tasks and managing error handling

The **block** directive groups related tasks and manages error handling, ensuring that tasks within the block are executed together and can handle failures gracefully.

Question 13: Which feature of Ansible allows you to reuse community-contributed roles?
A) Ansible Vault
B) Ansible Galaxy
C) Ansible Template
D) Ansible Block

Answer:
B) Ansible Galaxy

Ansible Galaxy allows you to reuse community-contributed roles, providing a repository of pre-built roles for various automation tasks.

Question 14: What is the primary use of the **AnsibleModule** class in custom modules?
A) To handle encryption and decryption
B) To manage arguments and results for the module
C) To create dynamic templates
D) To install community roles

Answer:
B) To manage arguments and results for the module

The **AnsibleModule** class manages arguments, validates input, and handles results for custom modules, ensuring proper interaction with Ansible.

Question 15: Which directive is used to skip tasks that do not need to be run, improving playbook efficiency?
A) **when**
B) **failed_when**
C) **async**
D) **changed_when**

Answer:
A) **when**

The **when** directive is used to conditionally skip tasks that do not need to be run, improving playbook efficiency by avoiding unnecessary operations.

Question 16: What does the **forks** configuration option in **ansible.cfg** control?
A) The number of parallel processes
B) The encryption method for sensitive data
C) The location of inventory files
D) The verbosity of playbook output

Answer:
A) The number of parallel processes

The **forks** configuration option controls the number of parallel processes, allowing more tasks to run simultaneously and speeding up playbook execution.

Question 17: Which Ansible directive is used to cache and reuse results of expensive operations?
A) **cache**
B) **block**
C) **register**
D) **fact_caching**

Answer:
D) **fact_caching**

Fact caching stores gathered facts about hosts, reducing the need to gather them every time a playbook runs, thus speeding up execution.

Question 18: What is the purpose of using **async** and **poll** in Ansible tasks?
A) To cache results of tasks
B) To run tasks asynchronously and check their status later
C) To encrypt sensitive data
D) To conditionally skip tasks

Answer:
B) To run tasks asynchronously and check their status later

Using **async** and **poll** allows tasks to run asynchronously, enabling other tasks to execute concurrently and improving overall playbook performance.

Question 19: What is the primary benefit of enabling SSH connection reuse in Ansible?
A) Increased security
B) Reduced overhead of establishing new connections for each task
C) Improved encryption for sensitive data
D) Simplified inventory management

Answer:
B) Reduced overhead of establishing new connections for each task

Enabling SSH connection reuse reduces the overhead of establishing new connections for each task, improving playbook execution speed.

Question 20: Which Ansible plugin provides detailed timing information for playbook tasks, helping identify performance bottlenecks?
A) **profile_tasks**
B) **callback_whitelist**
C) **async_status**
D) **fact_caching**

Answer:
A) **profile_tasks**

The **profile_tasks** plugin provides detailed timing information for playbook tasks, helping identify and address performance bottlenecks.

Chapter 5: Ansible Plugins and Modules

Introduction

In this chapter, you will explore Ansible's plugins and modules to discover its advanced capabilities. The functionality of Ansible is enhanced by these components, which enable you to personalize and improve your automation tasks. It all starts with getting your head around Ansible plugins and modules, their functions, and their place in the Ansible ecosystem. Subsequently, you will learn how to install and utilize community modules by utilizing the extensive collection of pre-built solutions that have been contributed by the Ansible community. Next, we go over the building of custom Ansible modules, which will allow you to develop solutions that are specifically designed to meet your specific requirements.

As well, the chapter will provide instructions on how to develop action plugins that will enable you to integrate custom logic into your playbooks. In order to retrieve dynamic data during the execution of a playbook, you will acquire a knack of using lookup plugins and implement filter plugins to modify the data to meet your specific needs. You can modify Ansible's ability to connect to remote systems by managing connections with connection plugins, and you can customize inventory data sourcing by developing inventory plugins.

At the chapter's conclusion, you will have a firm grasp of Ansible's plugins and modules, allowing you to tailor the automation framework to your specific needs.

Recipe #1: Understanding Ansible Plugins and Modules

Ansible Plugins Overview

Ansible plugins are pieces of code that augment Ansible's core functionality. They allow you to customize and extend the behavior of Ansible in various ways. Plugins are categorized into different types based on their functionality as below:

- **Action Plugins:** Action plugins allow you to add custom logic to tasks. They can modify the execution flow or add additional processing steps. For example, an action plugin might ensure certain preconditions are met before running a task.
- **Lookup Plugins:** Lookup plugins fetch data from external sources. This data can be used within your playbooks dynamically. For example, the **file** lookup plugin reads the contents of a file, and the **env** lookup plugin retrieves environment variables.
- **Filter Plugins:** Filter plugins process data within playbooks. They transform input data into the desired output format. Common filters include **default**, **length**, and **replace**.
- **Connection Plugins:** Connection plugins define how Ansible connects to remote systems. For example, the **ssh** connection plugin uses SSH to connect to hosts, while the **local** plugin runs tasks locally.

- **Inventory Plugins:** Inventory plugins allow Ansible to source inventory data from various locations and formats, such as cloud providers or custom databases.
- **Callback Plugins:** Callback plugins react to Ansible events, providing additional output or integrating with other systems. For example, the **mail** callback plugin sends email notifications.

Module Return Values

As learned previously, modules are standalone scripts that Ansible executes on remote systems to perform specific tasks, such as installing packages, managing files, or configuring services. While you've already explored about using and creating custom modules, this section will cover some additional aspects not previously learned.

Modules return JSON-formatted data that Ansible processes. This data typically includes:

- **Changed:** Indicates whether the module made any changes.
- **Failed:** Indicates if the module execution failed.
- **Specific Data:** Custom data relevant to the module's task, such as command output or resource status.

Each module has arguments that control its behavior. Properly documenting these arguments using Ansible's documentation format ensures that they are clearly understood and correctly used. This documentation is accessible through the **ansible-doc** command.

Here in this recipe, we try to understand Ansible plugins and uncover additional insights into Ansible modules that have not been covered in previous chapters.

List of Ansible Plugins

At first, to get a list of available plugins, you please use the **ansible-doc** command:

```
ansible-doc -t plugin -l
```

This command lists all available plugins by type.

Module Return Values and Arguments

Modules return structured JSON data that includes a **changed** status, indicating whether the module made any changes. They may also return additional data specific to the module's task.

Properly document module arguments using Ansible's standard format. This ensures clarity and usability. The **ansible-doc** command provides access to module documentation:

```
ansible-doc module_name
```

Putting Plugin into use

To illustrate the use of a plugin, consider a playbook that uses the **env** lookup plugin to retrieve an environment variable:

```
---

- name: Use Lookup Plugin

  hosts: localhost

  tasks:

    - name: Retrieve environment variable

      debug:

        msg: "Home directory is {{ lookup('env', 'HOME')
}}"
```

Save this playbook and run it:

```
ansible-playbook
~/GitforGits/playbooks/use_lookup_plugin.yml
```

The above sample code retrieves the **HOME** environment variable using the **env** lookup plugin and displays it. This recipe provided an overview of the various types of plugins and additional insights into Ansible modules, enhancing your ability to create powerful and flexible automation solutions.

Recipe #2: Installing and using Community Modules

Community modules are pre-built modules contributed by the Ansible community. These modules extend the functionality of Ansible, enabling you to perform a wide range of tasks without writing custom modules from scratch. Leveraging community modules can save time and effort, as well as ensure that you are following best practices established by other users.

In this recipe, you will learn to find, install, and use community modules in your Ansible playbooks.

Find and Install a Community Module

Community modules can be found on Ansible Galaxy. Visit the Ansible Galaxy website (https://galaxy.ansible.com/) and use the search functionality to find modules that match your needs. For example, if you need a module to manage Docker, you can search for "docker."

Use the **ansible-galaxy install** command to install a community module. For example, to install the **geerlingguy.docker** role, which includes Docker management modules:

```
ansible-galaxy install geerlingguy.docker
```

This command downloads the role and its associated modules to the **roles/** directory within your Ansible project. To put the community module into use, you first create a new playbook to use the installed community module as below:

```
nano ~/GitforGits/playbooks/use_docker_module.yml
```

Add the given below script to use the Docker module provided by the **geerlingguy.docker** role:

```
---

- name: Use Docker Community Module

  hosts: all

  become: yes

  roles:

    - geerlingguy.docker

  tasks:

    - name: Ensure Docker is running

      docker_container:
```

```
        name: nginx
        image: nginx
        state: started
        ports:
          - "80:80"
```

After running the playbook, check that the Docker container is running on the target hosts. SSH into one of the hosts and use the **docker ps** command:

```
ssh user@server1.gitforgits.com
docker ps
```

You should see the Nginx container listed and running.

You can also explore other community modules to find ones that suit your specific needs. Install and experiment with these modules to understand their capabilities and how they can be integrated into your playbooks.

Sample Program: Using 'geerlingguy.mysql' Role

To manage MySQL using a community module, you can install the **geerlingguy.mysql** role:

```
ansible-galaxy install geerlingguy.mysql
```

Create a new playbook to use the MySQL module:

```
nano ~/GitforGits/playbooks/use_mysql_module.yml
```

Add the script as given below:

```
---
- name: Use MySQL Community Module
  hosts: all
```

```
  become: yes
  roles:
    - geerlingguy.mysql
  tasks:
    - name: Ensure MySQL is running
      mysql_user:
        name: myuser
        password: mypassword
        priv: '*.*:ALL'
        state: present
```

Run the playbook:

```
ansible-playbook
~/GitforGits/playbooks/use_mysql_module.yml
```

These above steps help us to leverage community modules for saving time and effort by utilizing pre-built solutions, thereby allowing us to focus on specific automation needs.

Recipe #3: Writing Custom Ansible Modules

When the built-in modules or community-contributed roles do not cover your specific task, you will need to create custom Ansible modules. Here are a few examples of such uses:

- Custom modules can interface with proprietary APIs or systems that do not have existing Ansible modules.
- When a task involves multiple steps or complex logic, a custom module can encapsulate this complexity.
- Custom modules can handle intricate configuration tasks that require more control than what's offered by standard modules.

- Managing hardware with unique interfaces or protocols may require custom modules to communicate effectively.
- When specific data processing or transformation tasks are needed, a custom module can provide the necessary functionality.

In this recipe, you will learn to write custom Ansible modules to perform tasks that are not covered by existing modules.

Create Custom Module Script

Create a directory for your custom modules and a new Python script for your custom module:

```
mkdir -p ~/GitforGits/library

nano ~/GitforGits/library/custom_greeting.py
```

Add the given below script to the Python script:

```
#!/usr/bin/python


from ansible.module_utils.basic import AnsibleModule

def run_module():

    module_args = dict(

        name=dict(type='str', required=True)

    )


    result = dict(

        changed=False,

        original_message='',

        message=''
```

```
    )

    module = AnsibleModule(
        argument_spec=module_args,
        supports_check_mode=True
    )

    name = module.params['name']
    result['original_message'] = name
    result['message'] = f'Hello, {name}!'

    if module.check_mode:
        module.exit_json(**result)

    result['changed'] = True
    module.exit_json(**result)

def main():
    run_module()


if __name__ == '__main__':
```

```
main()
```

This simple custom module takes a **name** parameter and returns a greeting message. Now, ensure the custom module script is executable as below:

```
chmod +x ~/GitforGits/library/custom_greeting.py
```

Use Custom Module

Create a new playbook to use the custom module:

```
nano ~/GitforGits/playbooks/use_custom_greeting.yml
```

Add the script as given below:

```
---

- name: Use Custom Greeting Module

  hosts: localhost

  tasks:

    - name: Greet with custom module

      custom_greeting:

        name: Ansible

      register: result


    - name: Print result

      debug:

        var: result.message
```

After running the playbook, verify that the custom module executed correctly and printed the greeting message.

Sample Program: Managing a Custom Service

Create a new custom module to manage a hypothetical custom service. The above sample code will demonstrate more advanced features such as error handling and managing service states.

Create a new Python script for the custom service module:

```
nano ~/GitforGits/library/custom_service.py
```

Add the following script to the script:

```
#!/usr/bin/python


from ansible.module_utils.basic import AnsibleModule

import subprocess


def run_module():

    module_args = dict(

        name=dict(type='str', required=True),

        state=dict(type='str', required=True,
choices=['started', 'stopped'])

    )


    result = dict(

        changed=False,

        original_message='',
```

```
        message=''
    )

    module = AnsibleModule(
        argument_spec=module_args,
        supports_check_mode=True
    )

    name = module.params['name']
    state = module.params['state']

    result['original_message'] = name

    if state == 'started':
        try:
            subprocess.check_call(['systemctl', 'start',
name])
            result['changed'] = True
            result['message'] = f'Service {name} started'
        except subprocess.CalledProcessError as e:
            module.fail_json(msg=f'Failed to start
service {name}: {str(e)}', **result)
```

```
    elif state == 'stopped':
        try:
            subprocess.check_call(['systemctl', 'stop',
name])
            result['changed'] = True
            result['message'] = f'Service {name} stopped'
        except subprocess.CalledProcessError as e:
            module.fail_json(msg=f'Failed to stop service
{name}: {str(e)}', **result)

    if module.check_mode:
        module.exit_json(**result)

    module.exit_json(**result)

def main():
    run_module()

if __name__ == '__main__':
    main()
```

Ensure the custom module script is executable:

```
chmod +x ~/GitforGits/library/custom_service.py
```

Create a new playbook to use the custom service module:

```
nano ~/GitforGits/playbooks/manage_custom_service.yml
```

Add the script as given below:

```
---
- name: Manage Custom Service
 hosts: localhost
  tasks:
    - name: Start custom service
      custom_service:
        name: my_custom_service
        state: started
      register: result

    - name: Print result
      debug:
        var: result.message
```

Execute the playbook and then you have successfully written and used custom Ansible modules.

Recipe #4: Creating Action Plugins for Custom Logic

Action plugins allow you to extend the functionality of modules by adding custom logic to tasks. They enable you to manipulate data, execute additional logic, or modify the execution flow of tasks. Creating custom action plugins can significantly enhance the flexibility and power of your Ansible playbooks.

This recipe guides you to create and use custom action plugins to add custom logic to your Ansible tasks.

Create Custom Action Plugin Script

Before creating the custom script, make sure you have the necessary directory structure for your custom action plugins:

```
mkdir -p ~/GitforGits/action_plugins
```

Now, create a new Python script for your custom action plugin:

```
nano ~/GitforGits/action_plugins/custom_action.py
```

Add the following script to the script:

```
from ansible.plugins.action import ActionBase

from ansible.errors import AnsibleError


class ActionModule(ActionBase):

    def run(self, tmp=None, task_vars=None):

        # Retrieve parameters from the task

        result = super(ActionModule, self).run(tmp,
task_vars)

        module_args = self._task.args.copy()


        # Example custom logic: Validate input
```

```
        if 'message' not in module_args:
            raise AnsibleError("The 'message' parameter
is required")

        message = module_args['message']

        # Add custom logic here
        result['changed'] = True
        result['message'] = f"Custom Action: {message}"

        return result
```

This simple action plugin retrieves a **message** parameter, validates it, and processes it to return a custom message. And then, ensure the custom action plugin script is executable:

```
chmod +x ~/GitforGits/action_plugins/custom_action.py
```

Use Custom Action Plugin

Create a new playbook to use the custom action plugin:

```
nano ~/GitforGits/playbooks/use_custom_action.yml
```

Add the following code snippet:

```
---
- name: Use Custom Action Plugin
  hosts: localhost
```

```
  tasks:
    - name: Execute custom action
      custom_action:
        message: "Hello from the custom action plugin"
      register: result
    - name: Print result
      debug:
        var: result.message
```

After running the playbook, verify that the custom action plugin executed.

Sample Program: Adding Pre- and Post-Task Logic

Let us extend the custom action plugin to include pre- and post-task logic, such as logging or additional validation.

To do this, first open the custom action plugin script:

```
nano ~/GitforGits/action_plugins/custom_action.py
```

Modify the script to include pre- and post-task logic:

```
from ansible.plugins.action import ActionBase
from ansible.errors import AnsibleError


class ActionModule(ActionBase):
    def run(self, tmp=None, task_vars=None):
        result = super(ActionModule, self).run(tmp,
task_vars)
```

```
        module_args = self._task.args.copy()

        # Pre-task logic
        self._display.display("Executing custom action
plugin...")

        if 'message' not in module_args:
            raise AnsibleError("The 'message' parameter
is required")

        message = module_args['message']

        # Main task logic
        result['changed'] = True
        result['message'] = f"Custom Action: {message}"

        # Post-task logic
        self._display.display("Custom action plugin
execution complete.")

        return result
```

Ensure the custom action plugin script is executable:

```
chmod +x ~/GitforGits/action_plugins/custom_action.py
```

Re-run the playbook using the **ansible-playbook** command:

```
ansible-playbook
~/GitforGits/playbooks/use_custom_action.yml
```

With these steps, you have successfully created and used a custom action plugin to add complex logic and extend the functionality of your tasks.

Recipe #5: Using Lookup Plugins for Dynamic Data

Lookup plugins are used to fetch data from external sources dynamically during playbook execution. They allow you to retrieve information such as file contents, environment variables, or data from external databases and APIs. In this recipe, you will learn to use lookup plugins to fetch dynamic data during playbook execution, enhancing the flexibility and adaptability of your playbooks.

Understanding Lookup Plugins

Lookup plugins enable you to retrieve data from various sources. Some commonly used lookup plugins include:

- **file:** Reads the contents of a file.
- **env:** Retrieves the value of an environment variable.
- **url:** Fetches data from a URL.
- **csvfile:** Reads data from a CSV file.
- **password:** Generates or retrieves a password from a password file.

'file'

The **file** lookup plugin reads the contents of a file and returns it as a string. This can be useful for including configuration snippets or other data stored in files.

Try creating a sample file with some content:

```
echo "This is a sample file content" >
~/GitforGits/sample_file.txt
```

Then, create a new playbook to use the **file** lookup plugin:

```
nano ~/GitforGits/playbooks/use_file_lookup.yml
```

Add the following script to the playbook:

```
---

- name: Use File Lookup Plugin

  hosts: localhost

  tasks:

    - name: Read file content

      debug:

        msg: "{{ lookup('file', '../sample_file.txt') }}"
```

'env'

The **env** lookup plugin retrieves the value of an environment variable. This can be useful for accessing environment-specific configurations.

Now to use the **env** lookup plugin, create a new playbook:

```
nano ~/GitforGits/playbooks/use_env_lookup.yml
```

Add the following script to the playbook:

```
---

- name: Use Env Lookup Plugin

  hosts: localhost
```

```
  tasks:
    - name: Retrieve environment variable
      debug:
        msg: "Home directory is {{ lookup('env', 'HOME')
}}"
```

'url'

The **url** lookup plugin fetches data from a URL. This can be useful for retrieving dynamic content or configuration data from web services.

To use the **url** lookup plugin, create a new playbook and add the given below script to the playbook:

```
nano ~/GitforGits/playbooks/use_url_lookup.yml
---
- name: Use URL Lookup Plugin
  hosts: localhost
  tasks:
    - name: Fetch data from URL
      debug:
        msg: "{{ lookup('url', 'http://gitforgits.com')
}}"
```

'csvfile'

The **csvfile** lookup plugin reads data from a CSV file. This can be useful for processing structured data stored in CSV format.

Firstly, create a sample CSV file with some data:

```
echo "name,age\nRAMA,30\nKRISHNA,25" >
~/GitforGits/sample_data.csv
```

Create a new playbook:

```
nano ~/GitforGits/playbooks/use_csvfile_lookup.yml
```

Add the given below script to the playbook:

```
---

- name: Use CSVFile Lookup Plugin

  hosts: localhost

  tasks:

    - name: Read CSV data

      debug:

        msg: "{{ lookup('csvfile', '../sample_data.csv')
}}"
```

'password'

The **password** lookup plugin generates or retrieves a password from a password file. This is useful for managing passwords securely within playbooks.

Create a new playbook to use the **password** lookup plugin:

```
nano ~/GitforGits/playbooks/use_password_lookup.yml
```

Add the given below script to the playbook:

```
---

- name: Use Password Lookup Plugin
```

```
  hosts: localhost

  tasks:

    - name: Generate or retrieve password

      debug:

        msg: "{{ lookup('password',
'/path/to/password/file length=12 chars=ascii_letters')
}}"
```

Execute all the playbooks:

```
ansible-playbook
~/GitforGits/playbooks/use_file_lookup.yml

ansible-playbook
~/GitforGits/playbooks/use_env_lookup.yml

ansible-playbook
~/GitforGits/playbooks/use_url_lookup.yml

ansible-playbook
~/GitforGits/playbooks/use_csvfile_lookup.yml

ansible-playbook
~/GitforGits/playbooks/use_password_lookup.yml
```

This means that you have effectively used multiple lookup plugins to retrieve dynamic data while the playbook is running. You can easily retrieve and use data from diverse sources with lookup plugins, which enhance the adaptability and flexibility of your playbooks.

Recipe #6: Implementing Filter Plugins for Data Transformation

Data transformation involves manipulating data to fit specific formats, perform calculations, or apply custom logic. By transforming data, you can ensure that the information used in your playbooks is in the desired state, making your automation tasks more efficient and effective. Filter plugins allow you to process variables, modify their values, and generate new data based on existing inputs.

In this recipe, you will learn to create and use custom filter plugins to perform data transformation, ensuring that the data in your playbooks is properly formatted and ready for use.

Create Custom Filter Plugin Script

At first, ensure you have the necessary directory structure for your custom filter plugins:

```
mkdir -p ~/GitforGits/filter_plugins
```

Create a new Python script for your custom filter plugin:

```
nano ~/GitforGits/filter_plugins/custom_filters.py
```

Add the given below script to the Python script:

```
def to_uppercase(value):
    """Converts a string to uppercase."""
    if not isinstance(value, str):
        raise TypeError("Value must be a string")
    return value.upper()


class FilterModule(object):
    """Custom filters."""


    def filters(self):
        return {
```

```
        'to_uppercase': to_uppercase,
    }
```

This simple filter plugin converts a string to uppercase.

Use Custom Filter Plugin

Create a new playbook to use the custom filter plugin:

```
nano ~/GitforGits/playbooks/use_custom_filter.yml
```

Add the following code snippet:

```
---
- name: Use Custom Filter Plugin
  hosts: localhost
  tasks:
    - name: Apply custom filter
      debug:
        msg: "{{ 'hello world' | to_uppercase }}"
```

Execute the playbook and verify that the custom filter plugin executed correctly and transformed the string to uppercase.

Sample Program: Creating Complex Filters

Create additional filters for more complex data transformations. For example, a filter to calculate the factorial of a number and to do this, open the custom filter plugin script:

```
nano ~/GitforGits/filter_plugins/custom_filters.py
```

Modify the script to include the new filter:

```
def to_uppercase(value):
    """Converts a string to uppercase."""
    if not isinstance(value, str):
        raise TypeError("Value must be a string")
    return value.upper()


def factorial(n):
    """Calculates the factorial of a number."""
    if not isinstance(n, int) or n < 0:
        raise ValueError("Value must be a non-negative
integer")
    if n == 0 or n == 1:
        return 1
    else:
        return n * factorial(n - 1)


class FilterModule(object):
    """Custom filters."""

    def filters(self):
        return {
            'to_uppercase': to_uppercase,
```

```
        'factorial': factorial,
    }
```

Update the playbook to use the new filters:

```
nano ~/GitforGits/playbooks/use_custom_filter.yml
```

Modify the content to apply the new filters:

```
---
- name: Use Custom Filter Plugin
  hosts: localhost
  tasks:
    - name: Apply uppercase filter
      debug:
        msg: "{{ 'hello world' | to_uppercase }}"

    - name: Calculate factorial
      debug:
        msg: "Factorial of 5 is {{ 5 | factorial }}"
```

Re-run the playbook:

```
ansible-playbook
~/GitforGits/playbooks/use_custom_filter.yml
```

You can continue to add more complex data transformations as needed. For example, creating filters for data validation, formatting dates, or manipulating lists and dictionaries.

Sample Program: Date Formatting Filter

Update the custom filter plugin script to include a date formatting filter:

```
import datetime


def to_uppercase(value):
    """Converts a string to uppercase."""
    if not isinstance(value, str):
        raise TypeError("Value must be a string")
    return value.upper()


def factorial(n):
    """Calculates the factorial of a number."""
    if not isinstance(n, int) or n < 0:
        raise ValueError("Value must be a non-negative
integer")
    if n == 0 or n == 1:
        return 1
    else:
        return n * factorial(n - 1)


def format_date(value, date_format='%Y-%m-%d'):
    """Formats a date string to the specified format."""
```

```
    try:
        date_obj = datetime.datetime.strptime(value, '%Y-
%m-%d')
        return date_obj.strftime(date_format)
    except ValueError as e:
        raise ValueError(f"Invalid date format: {e}")

class FilterModule(object):
    """Custom filters."""

    def filters(self):
        return {
            'to_uppercase': to_uppercase,
            'factorial': factorial,
            'format_date': format_date,
        }
```

Update the playbook to use the date formatting filter:

```
nano ~/GitforGits/playbooks/use_custom_filter.yml
```

Modify the script:

```
---
- name: Use Custom Filter Plugin
```

```
  hosts: localhost

  tasks:

    - name: Apply uppercase filter

      debug:

        msg: "{{ 'hello world' | to_uppercase }}"


    - name: Calculate factorial

      debug:

        msg: "Factorial of 5 is {{ 5 | factorial }}"


    - name: Format date

      debug:

        msg: "Formatted date is {{ '2024-07-01' |
format_date('%B %d, %Y') }}"
```

Re-run the playbook and verify that the **to_uppercase**, **factorial**, and **format_date** filters executed correctly and transformed the data as expected. By following these steps, you have successfully created and used custom filter plugins to perform data transformations. Filter plugins enable you to manipulate and format data dynamically within your playbooks, enhancing the flexibility and power of your automation scripts.

Recipe #7: Managing Connections with Connection Plugins

Connection Plugins Overview

Connection plugins define how the control node connects to the managed nodes. These plugins handle the communication layer, ensuring that tasks are executed on the remote hosts. Different environments and requirements might necessitate using various connection types such as SSH, local, Docker, or custom protocols. By customizing connection plugins, you can optimize and secure the connection process based on your specific needs.

Our goal in this recipe is to use and create custom connection plugins to manage connections effectively, ensuring efficient and secure communication with remote hosts.

Understanding Built-in Connection Plugins

Ansible comes with several built-in connection plugins, including:

- **SSH:** The default method for connecting to remote hosts using SSH.
- **Local:** Executes tasks on the local machine where Ansible is running.
- **Docker:** Connects to Docker containers.
- **WinRM:** Connects to Windows hosts using the Windows Remote Management protocol.
- **Chroot:** Connects to a chroot jail.

You can list available connection plugins using the **ansible-doc** command:

```
ansible-doc -t connection -l
```

Using Built-in Connection Plugin

To use a built-in connection plugin, specify it in your playbook or inventory file. For example, to use the Docker connection plugin:

Inventory File Configuration

```
[webservers]

web1.gitforgits.com ansible_connection=docker

web2.gitforgits.com ansible_connection=docker
```

Playbook Configuration

```
---
```

```
- name: Use Docker Connection
  hosts: webservers
  tasks:
    - name: Ping Docker containers
      ping:
```

Creating Custom Connection Plugin

To create a custom connection plugin, you need to define a new connection plugin script. Custom connection plugins can be used to implement specific protocols or connection methods not covered by built-in plugins.

First, ensure you have the necessary directory structure for your custom connection plugins:

```
mkdir -p ~/GitforGits/connection_plugins
```

Create Custom Connection Plugin Script

Create a new Python script for your custom connection plugin:

```
nano ~/GitforGits/connection_plugins/custom_connection.py
```

Add the following script to the Python script:

```
from ansible.plugins.connection import ConnectionBase
from ansible.errors import AnsibleConnectionFailure
class Connection(ConnectionBase):
    ''' Custom connection plugin '''
    transport = 'custom'
    has_pipelining = True
```

```
    def __init__(self, *args, **kwargs):
        super(Connection, self).__init__(*args, **kwargs)

    def _connect(self):
        # Implement the connection logic
        if not self.connected:
            # Simulate connection logic (e.g., open a
socket, SSH, etc.)
            self.connected = True

    def exec_command(self, cmd, in_data=None,
sudoable=True):
        ''' Run a command on the remote host '''
        self._connect()
        if not self.connected:
            raise AnsibleConnectionFailure("Failed to
connect")

        # Simulate command execution
        result = {
            'rc': 0,
            'stdout': f"Executed: {cmd}",
```

```
            'stderr': '',
        }
        return result

    def put_file(self, in_path, out_path):
        ''' Transfer a file to the remote host '''
        self._connect()
        if not self.connected:
            raise AnsibleConnectionFailure("Failed to
connect")

        # Simulate file transfer
        with open(in_path, 'rb') as in_file:
            with open(out_path, 'wb') as out_file:
                out_file.write(in_file.read())

    def fetch_file(self, in_path, out_path):
        ''' Fetch a file from the remote host '''
        self._connect()
        if not self.connected:
            raise AnsibleConnectionFailure("Failed to
connect")
```

```
        # Simulate file fetching
        with open(in_path, 'rb') as in_file:
            with open(out_path, 'wb') as out_file:
                out_file.write(in_file.read())

    def close(self):
        ''' Close the connection '''
        if self.connected:
            self.connected = False
```

Use Custom Connection Plugin

Create a new playbook to use the custom connection plugin:

```
nano ~/GitforGits/playbooks/use_custom_connection.yml
```

Add the following code snippet:

```
---
- name: Use Custom Connection Plugin
  hosts: localhost
  tasks:
    - name: Execute custom connection command
      ping:
      vars:
```

```
    ansible_connection: custom
```

After running the playbook, verify that the custom connection plugin executed correctly and connected to the host. By now, you have successfully used and created custom connection plugins to manage connections effectively.

Recipe #8: Developing Inventory Plugins for Custom Sources

Our goal in this recipe is to develop custom inventory plugins to source inventory data from custom sources, enhancing the flexibility and adaptability of your Ansible automation.

Inventory Plugins Overview

Inventory plugins allow you to source inventory data from various locations and formats, such as cloud providers, databases, or custom data sources. Inventory plugins enable Ansible to retrieve host and group information dynamically. Built-in plugins support various sources like AWS, GCP, and OpenStack, but custom plugins can be created to integrate with other sources.

Create Custom Inventory Plugin Script

Create a new Python script for your custom inventory plugin:

```
nano ~/GitforGits/inventory_plugins/custom_inventory.py
```

Add the given below script to the Python script:

```
import json

from ansible.plugins.inventory import BaseInventoryPlugin

from ansible.errors import AnsibleParserError


DOCUMENTATION = '''

    name: custom_inventory
```

```
    plugin_type: inventory
    short_description: Custom inventory source
    description:
        - This is a custom inventory plugin for Ansible
    options:
        plugin:
            description: Name of the plugin
            required: True
            choices: ['custom_inventory']
'''

class InventoryModule(BaseInventoryPlugin):

    NAME = 'custom_inventory'

    def verify_file(self, path):
        ''' Verify if the provided file is a valid source
'''
        valid = super(InventoryModule,
self).verify_file(path)
        if valid:
```

```
        if path.endswith(('custom_inventory.yml',
'custom_inventory.yaml')):
            return True
        return False

    def parse(self, inventory, loader, path, cache=True):
        ''' Parse the inventory file '''
        super(InventoryModule, self).parse(inventory,
loader, path)

        # Read the inventory configuration
        config = self._read_config_data(path)

        # Validate required options
        if 'hosts' not in config:
            raise AnsibleParserError('The "hosts" option
is required')

        # Add hosts and groups from the custom source
        for host in config['hosts']:
            self.inventory.add_host(host)
            for group in
config['hosts'][host].get('groups', []):
```

```
                self.inventory.add_group(group)

                self.inventory.add_host(host, group)


            # Add host variables

            for var, value in
config['hosts'][host].get('vars', {}).items():

                self.inventory.set_variable(host, var,
value)
```

Create Inventory Configuration File

Create an inventory configuration file that defines the custom source data:

```
nano ~/GitforGits/inventory/custom_inventory.yml
```

Add the following code snippet:

```
plugin: custom_inventory

hosts:

  web1.gitforgits.com:

    groups:

      - webservers

    vars:

      ansible_host: 192.168.1.101

  web2.gitforgits.com:

    groups:
```

```
      - webservers
    vars:
      ansible_host: 192.168.1.102
  db1.gitforgits.com:
    groups:
      - databases
    vars:
      ansible_host: 192.168.1.201
```

Use Custom Inventory Plugin

Create a new playbook to use the custom inventory plugin:

```
nano ~/GitforGits/playbooks/use_custom_inventory.yml
```

Add the following code snippet:

```
---
- name: Use Custom Inventory Plugin
  hosts: all
  tasks:
    - name: Ping all hosts
      ping:
```

Revising Inventory File

Add the given below script to the inventory file that existingly includes the custom inventory plugin:

```
[all:vars]

ansible_inventory_enabled_plugins = custom_inventory
```

While executing, specify the custom inventory configuration file:

```
ansible-playbook -i
~/GitforGits/inventory/custom_inventory.yml
~/GitforGits/playbooks/use_custom_inventory.yml
```

After running the playbook, verify that the custom inventory plugin executed correctly and connected to the specified hosts.

Sample Program: Extending Custom Inventory Plugin

Open the custom inventory plugin script:

```
nano ~/GitforGits/inventory_plugins/custom_inventory.py
```

Modify the script to include logic for fetching data from an external API:

```
import json

import requests

from ansible.plugins.inventory import BaseInventoryPlugin

from ansible.errors import AnsibleParserError

DOCUMENTATION = '''

    name: custom_inventory

    plugin_type: inventory

    short_description: Custom inventory source

    description:

        - This is a custom inventory plugin for Ansible
```

```
    options:
        plugin:
            description: Name of the plugin
            required: True
            choices: ['custom_inventory']
        api_endpoint:
            description: API endpoint for fetching
inventory data
            required: True
'''

class InventoryModule(BaseInventoryPlugin):

    NAME = 'custom_inventory'

    def verify_file(self, path):
        ''' Verify if the provided file is a valid source
'''
        valid = super(InventoryModule,
self).verify_file(path)
        if valid:
            if path.endswith(('custom_inventory.yml',
'custom_inventory.yaml')):
```

```
                return True
        return False

    def parse(self, inventory, loader, path, cache=True):
        ''' Parse the inventory file '''
        super(InventoryModule, self).parse(inventory,
loader, path)

        # Read the inventory configuration
        config = self._read_config_data(path)

        # Validate required options
        if 'api_endpoint' not in config:
            raise AnsibleParserError('The "api_endpoint"
option is required')
        # Fetch inventory data from the API
        response = requests.get(config['api_endpoint'])
        if response.status_code != 200:
            raise AnsibleParserError(f"Failed to fetch
inventory data from {config['api_endpoint']}")

        inventory_data = response.json()
```

```
    # Add hosts and groups from the API response
    for host in inventory_data['hosts']:
        self.inventory.add_host(host)
        for group in
inventory_data['hosts'][host].get('groups', []):
            self.inventory.add_group(group)
            self.inventory.add_host(host, group)

        # Add host variables
        for var, value in
inventory_data['hosts'][host].get('vars', {}).items():
            self.inventory.set_variable(host, var,
value)
```

Update the inventory configuration file to include the API endpoint:

```
nano ~/GitforGits/inventory/custom_inventory.yml
```

Modify the script:

```
plugin: custom_inventory
api_endpoint: 'http://gitforgits.com/api/inventory'
```

Re-run the playbook and specify the custom inventory configuration file:

```
ansible-playbook -i
~/GitforGits/inventory/custom_inventory.yml
~/GitforGits/playbooks/use_custom_inventory.yml
```

Then, execute the playbook and verify that the custom inventory plugin fetched data from the external API and connected to the specified hosts.

Summary

This chapter taught you how to install and use Ansible Galaxy community modules, which allow you to save time and effort by utilizing the community's extensive library of pre-built solutions. The chapter addressed the development of custom Ansible modules to implement tasks that are not addressed by preexisting modules. You gained the knowledge of constructing custom modules to execute specific tasks, such as integrating with proprietary systems or managing a service. You also learned the development of action plugins, which enable you to incorporate custom logic into tasks, thereby increasing the flexibility and power of your playbooks.

Another significant topic was the utilization of lookup plugins for dynamic data. You learned how to get data from different places, like files, environment variables, URLs, and CSV files. This lets your playbooks adapt to new data sources and environments. Additionally, the implementation of filter plugins for data transformation was discussed, which illustrated the dynamic manipulation and formatting of data within playbooks.

This chapter also covered the management of connections using connection plugins, which is necessary for the creation and implementation of custom connection plugins to enhance and secure the communication process between the control node and managed nodes. Lastly, you created inventory plugins for custom sources, which allowed Ansible to retrieve inventory data from a variety of locations and formats, including external APIs and databases.

In sum, you should now be able to build more versatile, efficient, and powerful automation solutions thanks to the information you gained in this chapter about how to add plugins and modules to Ansible and modify its functionality.

Knowledge Exercise

Question 1: What is the primary purpose of action plugins in Ansible?
A) To manage inventory data
B) To add custom logic to tasks
C) To fetch data from external sources
D) To transform data within playbooks

Answer:
B) To add custom logic to tasks

Action plugins in Ansible are used to extend the functionality of modules by adding custom logic to tasks.

Question 2: Which command is used to list available connection plugins in Ansible?
A) **ansible-plugins list connection**
B) **ansible-doc -t connection -l**
C) **ansible-inventory --list**
D) **ansible-playbook --list-plugins**

Answer:
B) **ansible-doc -t connection -l**

The **ansible-doc -t connection -l** command lists all available connection plugins in Ansible.

Question 3: Which plugin type allows Ansible to retrieve host and group information dynamically?
A) Callback plugins
B) Lookup plugins
C) Inventory plugins
D) Action plugins

Answer:
C) Inventory plugins

Inventory plugins in Ansible enable it to retrieve host and group information dynamically from various sources.

Question 4: What is the purpose of the **verify_file** method in a custom inventory plugin?
A) To validate the inventory configuration file
B) To fetch data from external APIs
C) To execute commands on remote hosts
D) To transform data within playbooks

Answer:
A) To validate the inventory configuration file

The **verify_file** method in a custom inventory plugin is used to validate the inventory configuration file and ensure it is a valid source.

Question 5: Which plugin type is used to manipulate and format data within Ansible playbooks?
A) Action plugins
B) Connection plugins
C) Filter plugins
D) Lookup plugins

Answer:
C) Filter plugins

Filter plugins in Ansible are used to manipulate and format data within playbooks, enabling complex data transformations.

Question 6: What parameter is required to create a custom Ansible module that greets a user by name?
A) **username**
B) **greet**
C) **name**
D) **message**

Answer:
C) **name**

The **name** parameter is required to create a custom Ansible module that greets a user by name.

Question 7: Which lookup plugin would you use to read the contents of a file in Ansible?
A) **url**
B) **env**
C) **file**
D) **csvfile**

Answer:
C) **file**

The **file** lookup plugin in Ansible reads the contents of a file and returns it as a string.

Question 8: How do you specify the use of a custom connection plugin in an inventory file?
A) **ansible_connection: custom**
B) **connection: custom**
C) **custom_connection: true**
D) **use_connection: custom**

Answer:
A) **ansible_connection: custom**

To specify the use of a custom connection plugin in an inventory file, you use the **ansible_connection** parameter.

Question 9: Which method in a custom filter plugin is used to register the filters?
A) **get_filters**
B) **list_filters**
C) **filter**
D) **filters**

Answer:
D) **filters**

The **filters** method in a custom filter plugin is used to register the filters.

Question 10: What is the primary benefit of using community modules from Ansible Galaxy?
A) To fetch data from external APIs
B) To reuse pre-built solutions and save time
C) To transform data within playbooks
D) To execute custom commands on remote hosts

Answer:
B) To reuse pre-built solutions and save time

The primary benefit of using community modules from Ansible Galaxy is to reuse pre-built solutions and save time, leveraging the expertise of the Ansible community.

Question 11: Which of the following describes the main role of lookup plugins in Ansible?
A) They provide additional output for playbook execution.
B) They retrieve dynamic data from external sources.
C) They manage connection parameters.
D) They encrypt sensitive data.

Answer:
B) They retrieve dynamic data from external sources.

Lookup plugins in Ansible are used to fetch dynamic data from various sources, such as files, environment variables, and URLs, during playbook execution.

Question 12: What is the function of the **parse** method in a custom inventory plugin?
A) To validate input parameters.
B) To fetch and process inventory data.
C) To apply filters to data.
D) To execute remote commands.

Answer:
B) To fetch and process inventory data.

The **parse** method in a custom inventory plugin is responsible for fetching and processing inventory data, adding hosts and groups to the inventory.

Question 13: How can filter plugins enhance the flexibility of Ansible playbooks?
A) By encrypting sensitive variables.
B) By adding custom logic to tasks.
C) By transforming data dynamically.
D) By managing connection settings.

Answer:
C) By transforming data dynamically.

Filter plugins enhance the flexibility of Ansible playbooks by enabling dynamic data transformations, allowing you to manipulate and format data as needed.

Question 14: What command is used to install a role from Ansible Galaxy?
A) **ansible-galaxy get role_name**
B) **ansible-galaxy fetch role_name**
C) **ansible-galaxy install role_name**
D) **ansible-galaxy add role_name**

Answer:
C) **ansible-galaxy install role_name**

The **ansible-galaxy install role_name** command is used to install a role from Ansible Galaxy.

Question 15: Which built-in connection plugin is used to execute tasks on the local machine?
A) **ssh**
B) **local**
C) **docker**
D) **chroot**

Answer:
B) **local**

The **local** connection plugin in Ansible is used to execute tasks on the local machine where Ansible is running.

Question 16: What is a common use case for developing a custom action plugin in Ansible?
A) To manage inventory data.
B) To handle complex data transformations.
C) To add pre- and post-task logic.
D) To fetch dynamic data from APIs.

Answer:
C) To add pre- and post-task logic.

A common use case for developing a custom action plugin in Ansible is to add pre- and post-task logic, extending the functionality of modules.

Question 17: Which method in a custom connection plugin is responsible for executing commands on remote hosts?
A) **exec_task**
B) **run_command**
C) **exec_command**
D) **execute**

Answer:
C) **exec_command**

The **exec_command** method in a custom connection plugin is responsible for executing commands on remote hosts.

Question 18: What is the purpose of the **DOCUMENTATION** variable in a custom inventory plugin?
A) To store dynamic data fetched from external sources.
B) To define the plugin's metadata and configuration options.
C) To manage connection settings.
D) To apply filters to data.

Answer:
B) To define the plugin's metadata and configuration options.

The **DOCUMENTATION** variable in a custom inventory plugin is used to define the plugin's metadata and configuration options, providing necessary details for its usage.

Question 19: Which of the following is a benefit of using custom filter plugins in Ansible?
A) They encrypt playbook data.
B) They extend the functionality of modules.
C) They provide additional output for playbook execution.
D) They enable complex data manipulations and transformations.

Answer:
D) They enable complex data manipulations and transformations.

Custom filter plugins in Ansible enable complex data manipulations and transformations, allowing for greater flexibility in playbook data handling.

Question 20: What is the key advantage of using inventory plugins for dynamic inventory management?
A) They automate playbook execution.
B) They fetch inventory data from various sources automatically.
C) They manage SSH connections.
D) They handle data encryption.

Answer:
B) They fetch inventory data from various sources automatically.

The key advantage of using inventory plugins for dynamic inventory management is their ability to fetch inventory data from various sources automatically, ensuring that the inventory is always up-to-date.

Chapter 6: Provisioning on Windows and Mac Systems

Introduction

In the prior chapter, you learned how to extend and customize Ansible's capabilities by exploring the power of plugins and modules. This chapter starts off with the configuration of Ansible to function with Windows hosts, a critical action in the expansion of your automation capabilities to a new platform. You will acquire the ability to manage Windows hosts, which includes the utilization of WinRM (Windows Remote Management) to facilitate communication between Ansible and Windows systems. Furthermore, you will hands-on the installation of software and the configuration of services on Windows using Ansible, thereby enhancing the versatility and power of your automation.

Moving forward, you will configure Ansible to efficiently manage these hosts on Mac systems. You will acquire the ability to automate a variety of tasks on Mac systems, such as software installation and configuration. By following these recipes, you will acquire the ability to seamlessly manage both Windows and Mac environments, thereby incorporating them into your current automation workflows.

Recipe #1: Setting up Ansible for Windows

Installing Ansible on Linux, our default environment, is straightforward and well-documented. The process typically involves using a package manager like **apt** on Ubuntu or **yum** on CentOS to install Ansible directly from the official repositories. This simplicity and ease of installation have allowed us to quickly set up and start using Ansible for various automation tasks on Linux.

However, managing Windows hosts with Ansible requires a different approach, as Ansible runs on a Linux control node but can manage Windows machines remotely. To achieve this, we need to set up the control node to communicate with Windows hosts using WinRM (Windows Remote Management).

The objective of this recipe is to set up Ansible for managing Windows hosts by configuring the necessary components on the Windows machine and the Linux control node.

Install Ansible on Linux Control Node

To install Ansible on your Linux control node, use the package manager appropriate such as:

```
sudo apt update

sudo apt install ansible -y
```

Prepare Windows Host

To allow Ansible to manage a Windows host, you need to configure the Windows machine to accept remote management via WinRM.

Enable WinRM on Windows Host

Run the following commands in an elevated PowerShell prompt on the Windows machine:

```
winrm quickconfig

winrm set winrm/config/client/auth @{Basic="true"}

winrm set winrm/config/service/auth @{Basic="true"}

winrm set winrm/config/service @{AllowUnencrypted="true"}
```

Create User for Ansible Management

Create a user account on the Windows machine that Ansible will use to connect and manage the system. Ensure this user has the necessary administrative privileges.

Install pywinrm

Install the **pywinrm** library on your Linux control node to enable Ansible to communicate with Windows hosts using WinRM:

```
sudo pip install pywinrm
```

Update the Ansible inventory file to include the Windows host and specify the connection parameters:

```
[windows]

windows_host ansible_host=<WINDOWS_HOST_IP>
ansible_user=<USERNAME> ansible_password=<PASSWORD>
ansible_connection=winrm ansible_winrm_transport=basic
ansible_winrm_server_cert_validation=ignore
```

Replace **<WINDOWS_HOST_IP>**, **<USERNAME>**, and **<PASSWORD>** with the appropriate values for your Windows host. Then, create a simple Ansible playbook to test the connection to the Windows host:

```
nano ~/GitforGits/playbooks/test_windows_connection.yml
```

Add the following code snippet:

```
---

- name: Test Connection to Windows Host

  hosts: windows

  tasks:

    - name: Ping the Windows host

      win_ping:
```

Run the playbook using the **ansible-playbook** command:

```
ansible-playbook
~/GitforGits/playbooks/test_windows_connection.yml
```

If the setup is correct, you should see a successful response indicating that Ansible can communicate with the Windows host.

Recipe #2: Managing Windows Hosts

Once you have set up Ansible to manage Windows hosts, you can begin performing various administrative tasks on these hosts using Ansible playbooks. Managing Windows hosts with Ansible allows you to automate routine tasks, enforce configurations, and ensure consistency across your Windows infrastructure.

In this recipe, you will learn to manage Windows hosts using Ansible by performing common administrative tasks, such as checking system information, managing files, and creating users.

To begin with, create a playbook to gather system information from the Windows host:

```
nano ~/GitforGits/playbooks/windows_system_info.yml
```

Add the following code snippet:

```
---

- name: Gather System Information

  hosts: windows

  tasks:

    - name: Gather facts about the Windows host

      win_fact:
```

Run the playbook to gather system information:

```
ansible-playbook
~/GitforGits/playbooks/windows_system_info.yml
```

This playbook uses the **win_fact** module to gather information about the Windows host, such as operating system version, hardware details, and more.

Manage Files on Windows

Create a playbook to manage files on the Windows host, such as creating, deleting, and copying files:

```
nano ~/GitforGits/playbooks/windows_manage_files.yml
```

Add the script as given below:

```
---

- name: Manage Files on Windows

  hosts: windows

  tasks:

    - name: Create a directory

      win_file:
```

```
        path: C:\example
        state: directory

    - name: Create a file
      win_copy:
        content: "This is a test file."
        dest: C:\example\testfile.txt

    - name: Delete a file
      win_file:
        path: C:\example\testfile.txt
        state: absent
```

Run the playbook to manage files on the Windows host:

```
ansible-playbook
~/GitforGits/playbooks/windows_manage_files.yml
```

This playbook uses the **win_file** and **win_copy** modules to create a directory, create a file with specific content, and delete a file.

Create and Manage Users

Create a playbook to create and manage users on the Windows host:

```
nano ~/GitforGits/playbooks/windows_manage_users.yml
```

Add the script as given below:

```
---
- name: Manage Users on Windows
  hosts: windows
  tasks:
    - name: Create a user
      win_user:
        name: exampleuser
        password: Password123
        state: present

    - name: Ensure user is a member of the Administrators group
      win_group_membership:
        name: Administrators
        members: exampleuser
        state: present
```

Run the playbook to manage users on the Windows host:

```
ansible-playbook ~/GitforGits/playbooks/windows_manage_users.yml
```

This playbook uses the **win_user** and **win_group_membership** modules to create a user and ensure that the user is a member of the Administrators group.

Manage Windows Services

Create a playbook to manage Windows services:

```
nano ~/GitforGits/playbooks/windows_manage_services.yml
```

Add the following code snippet:

```
---
- name: Manage Windows Services
  hosts: windows
  tasks:
    - name: Ensure the Windows Update service is running
      win_service:
        name: wuauserv
        start_mode: auto
        state: started
```

Run the playbook to manage Windows services:

```
ansible-playbook
~/GitforGits/playbooks/windows_manage_services.yml
```

This playbook uses the **win_service** module to ensure that the Windows Update service is running and set to start automatically.

Install Software on Windows

Create a playbook to install software on the Windows host:

```
nano ~/GitforGits/playbooks/windows_install_software.yml
```

Add the script as given below:

```
---
- name: Install Software on Windows
  hosts: windows
  tasks:
    - name: Install Google Chrome
      win_chocolatey:
        name: googlechrome
        state: present
```

Run the playbook to install software on the Windows host:

```
ansible-playbook
~/GitforGits/playbooks/windows_install_software.yml
```

This playbook uses the **win_chocolatey** module to install Google Chrome using the Chocolatey package manager. By now, you have successfully managed Windows hosts using Ansible. These examples demonstrate to perform common administrative tasks, such as checking system information, managing files, creating users, managing services, and installing software.

Recipe #3: Using WinRM for Windows Communication

WinRM (Windows Remote Management) is a Microsoft protocol that allows remote management of Windows machines. It is a crucial component for managing Windows hosts with Ansible, enabling Ansible to execute tasks and gather information from Windows systems. Setting up and using WinRM correctly is essential for effective communication between your Ansible control node and Windows hosts.

This recipe guides you to configure and use WinRM for communication between Ansible and Windows hosts, ensuring secure and reliable remote management.

Configure WinRM on the Windows Host

To enable WinRM on the Windows host, you need to configure it to accept remote management commands.

Enable WinRM

Run the following commands in an elevated PowerShell prompt on the Windows machine:

```
winrm quickconfig

winrm set winrm/config/client/auth @{Basic="true"}

winrm set winrm/config/service/auth @{Basic="true"}

winrm set winrm/config/service @{AllowUnencrypted="true"}
```

Set Trusted Hosts

If your Ansible control node and Windows host are not in the same domain, you may need to set the Ansible control node as a trusted host. Run this command in PowerShell:

```
winrm set winrm/config/client @{TrustedHosts="*"}
```

Replace "*" with the specific IP address or hostname of your Ansible control node if you prefer a more secure setup.

Configure Ansible Inventory

Add the following code to the inventory file, replacing the placeholders with your actual Windows host details:

```
[windows]

windows_host ansible_host=<WINDOWS_HOST_IP>
ansible_user=<USERNAME> ansible_password=<PASSWORD>
ansible_connection=winrm ansible_winrm_transport=basic
ansible_winrm_server_cert_validation=ignore
```

Test WinRM Connection

Create a simple Ansible playbook to test the WinRM connection:

```
nano ~/GitforGits/playbooks/test_winrm_connection.yml
```

Add the following code snippet:

```
---

- name: Test WinRM Connection

  hosts: windows

  tasks:

    - name: Ping the Windows host

      win_ping:
```

Run the playbook to test the connection:

```
ansible-playbook
~/GitforGits/playbooks/test_winrm_connection.yml
```

If the setup is correct, you should see a successful response indicating that Ansible can communicate with the Windows host via WinRM.

Securing WinRM Communication

For a production environment, it is recommended to secure WinRM communication using HTTPS. This involves generating and installing a self-signed certificate or obtaining a certificate from a trusted Certificate Authority (CA).

Generate a Self-Signed Certificate

Run the following commands in an elevated PowerShell prompt on the Windows host:

```
$cert = New-SelfSignedCertificate -CertStoreLocation
Cert:\LocalMachine\My -DnsName "winrm.gitforgits.com"

New-Item -Path WSMan:\Localhost\ClientCertificate -Value
@{Issuer = $cert.Issuer; Subject = $cert.Subject}
```

```
winrm create
winrm/config/listener?Address=*+Transport=HTTPS
@{"Hostname"="winrm.gitforgits.com";
"CertificateThumbprint"="$($cert.Thumbprint)"}
```

Update Ansible Inventory for HTTPS

Update your Ansible inventory file to use HTTPS for WinRM communication:

```
[windows]

windows_host ansible_host=<WINDOWS_HOST_IP>
ansible_user=<USERNAME> ansible_password=<PASSWORD>
ansible_connection=winrm ansible_winrm_transport=ntlm
ansible_winrm_server_cert_validation=ignore
ansible_port=5986
```

Once WinRM is configured and tested, you can use it to manage various aspects of Windows hosts through Ansible playbooks.

Sample Program: Managing Windows Services

Create a playbook to manage a Windows service using WinRM:

```
nano ~/GitforGits/playbooks/manage_windows_service.yml
```

Add the following code snippet:

```
---

- name: Manage Windows Service

  hosts: windows

  tasks:

    - name: Ensure Windows Update service is running

      win_service:
```

```
        name: wuauserv

        start_mode: auto

        state: started
```

Run the playbook to manage the Windows service:

```
ansible-playbook
~/GitforGits/playbooks/manage_windows_service.yml
```

By following these steps, you have successfully configured and used WinRM for communication between Ansible and Windows hosts. This setup enables you to manage and automate tasks on Windows machines, integrating them seamlessly into your Ansible workflows.

Recipe #4: Installing Software on Windows with Ansible

Managing software installations on Windows hosts can be efficiently handled using Ansible. By automating software installation, you can ensure consistency across your Windows infrastructure, save time, and reduce errors. Ansible provides several modules to manage software installations on Windows, including the **win_chocolatey** module for installing packages from the Chocolatey package manager.

In this recipe, you will learn to use Ansible to install software on Windows hosts, leveraging the **win_chocolatey** module and other relevant modules.

Install Chocolatey on Windows Host

Chocolatey is a popular package manager for Windows. First, you need to install Chocolatey on your Windows host. Run the following command in an elevated PowerShell prompt:

```
Set-ExecutionPolicy Bypass -Scope Process -Force;
[System.Net.ServicePointManager]::SecurityProtocol =
[System.Net.ServicePointManager]::SecurityProtocol -bor
3072; iex ((New-Object
System.Net.WebClient).DownloadString('https://community.c
hocolatey.org/install.ps1'))
```

Configure Ansible Inventory

Replace **<WINDOWS_HOST_IP>**, **<USERNAME>**, and **<PASSWORD>** with the appropriate values for your Windows host.

```
 [windows]

windows_host ansible_host=<WINDOWS_HOST_IP>
ansible_user=<USERNAME> ansible_password=<PASSWORD>
ansible_connection=winrm ansible_winrm_transport=basic
ansible_winrm_server_cert_validation=ignore
```

Install Software

Create a new playbook to install software on the Windows host using Chocolatey:

```
nano ~/GitforGits/playbooks/install_software_windows.yml
```

Add the following code snippet:

```
---

- name: Install Software on Windows

  hosts: windows

  tasks:

    - name: Ensure Chocolatey is installed

      win_chocolatey:

        name: chocolatey

        state: present


    - name: Install Google Chrome
```

```
      win_chocolatey:
        name: googlechrome
        state: present

    - name: Install 7-Zip
      win_chocolatey:
        name: 7zip
        state: present
```

This playbook ensures that Chocolatey is installed on the Windows host and then uses Chocolatey to install Google Chrome and 7-Zip.

After the playbook has run, verify that the software has been installed on the Windows host. You can check this by logging into the Windows machine and looking for the installed applications or by running specific commands to verify their presence.

Sample Program: Installing Additional Software

To install additional software, you can modify the playbook to include more packages. For example, to install Notepad++ and VLC Media Player, update the playbook as follows:

```
nano ~/GitforGits/playbooks/install_software_windows.yml
```

Add the following tasks:

```
---
- name: Install Software on Windows
  hosts: windows
  tasks:
    - name: Ensure Chocolatey is installed
```

```
    win_chocolatey:
      name: chocolatey
      state: present

  - name: Install Google Chrome
    win_chocolatey:
      name: googlechrome
      state: present

  - name: Install 7-Zip
    win_chocolatey:
      name: 7zip
      state: present

  - name: Install Notepad++
    win_chocolatey:
      name: notepadplusplus
      state: present

  - name: Install VLC Media Player
    win_chocolatey:
```

```
        name: vlc

        state: present
```

Execute the updated playbook using the **ansible-playbook** command:

```
ansible-playbook
~/GitforGits/playbooks/install_software_windows.yml
```

After running the updated playbook, verify that Notepad++ and VLC Media Player have been installed on the Windows host. This approach allows you to automate software installations, ensuring consistency and efficiency across your Windows infrastructure.

Recipe #5: Configuring Windows Services

Managing and configuring Windows services is a common administrative task that can be automated using Ansible. By using Ansible's **win_service** module, you can start, stop, enable, disable, and configure Windows services efficiently.

Our goal in this recipe is to use Ansible to manage Windows services, including starting, stopping, enabling, and configuring services on Windows hosts.

To begin with, check that the Ansible inventory includes the Windows host details. If you haven't configured it yet, you can refer to the inventory setup as directed in Recipe #1 of this chapter.

Manage Windows Services

Create a new playbook to manage Windows services. Open your playbook file:

```
nano ~/GitforGits/playbooks/manage_windows_services.yml
```

Add the given below script to manage different services:

```
---

- name: Manage Windows Services

  hosts: windows

  tasks:
```

```yaml
    - name: Ensure Windows Update service is running
      win_service:
        name: wuauserv
        start_mode: auto
        state: started

    - name: Stop and disable Print Spooler service
      win_service:
        name: Spooler
        start_mode: disabled
        state: stopped

    - name: Restart the DNS Client service
      win_service:
        name: Dnscache
        state: restarted

    - name: Ensure Windows Defender service is enabled
and running
      win_service:
        name: WinDefend
        start_mode: auto
```

```
        state: started
```

After the playbook has run, verify that the services have been configured correctly on the Windows host. You can do this by logging into the Windows machine and checking the status of the services using the Services console or the PowerShell **Get-Service** cmdlet.

Sample Program: Additional Service Management

To manage additional services, you can modify the playbook to include more tasks. For example, to start the Remote Desktop Services and stop the Windows Error Reporting Service, update the playbook as follows:

```
nano ~/GitforGits/playbooks/manage_windows_services.yml
```

Add the following tasks:

```
---

- name: Manage Windows Services

  hosts: windows

  tasks:

    - name: Ensure Windows Update service is running

      win_service:

        name: wuauserv

        start_mode: auto

        state: started


    - name: Stop and disable Print Spooler service

      win_service:

        name: Spooler
```

```
        start_mode: disabled

        state: stopped

    - name: Restart the DNS Client service

      win_service:

        name: Dnscache

        state: restarted


    - name: Ensure Windows Defender service is enabled
and running

      win_service:

        name: WinDefend

        start_mode: auto

        state: started


    - name: Start Remote Desktop Services

      win_service:

        name: TermService

        start_mode: auto

        state: started


    - name: Stop Windows Error Reporting Service
```

```
    win_service:
      name: WerSvc
      state: stopped
```

Execute the updated playbook using the **ansible-playbook** command:

```
ansible-playbook
~/GitforGits/playbooks/manage_windows_services.yml
```

After running the updated playbook, verify that the additional services have been managed correctly on the Windows host.

Recipe #6: Setting up Ansible for Mac

Managing Mac systems using Ansible involves setting up the control node and the Mac hosts for seamless automation. This recipe directs you through configuring your Mac systems to be managed by Ansible, similar to how you manage Linux and Windows hosts.

In this recipe, you will learn to set up Ansible to manage Mac systems, including installing necessary dependencies and configuring SSH access for Ansible to communicate with Mac hosts.

Prepare the Mac Host

Ensure the Mac host is configured to accept SSH connections, which is the default method Ansible uses to communicate with remote hosts.

Enable Remote Login

On the Mac host, enable remote login to allow SSH connections:

1. Open "System Preferences" on the Mac host.
2. Go to "Sharing."
3. Check the box next to "Remote Login" to enable SSH access.

Create a User for Ansible Management

Create a user account on the Mac host that Ansible will use to connect and manage the system. Ensure this user has the necessary administrative privileges.

Setup SSH Key-based Authentication

To enable Ansible to communicate securely with the Mac host, set up SSH key-based authentication.

Generate SSH Key Pair

On your control node, generate an SSH key pair if you don't already have one:

```
ssh-keygen -t rsa -b 4096
```

Copy SSH Public Key to Mac Host

Copy the SSH public key to the Mac host. Replace **<USERNAME>** and **<MAC_HOST_IP>** with the appropriate values for your Mac host:

```
ssh-copy-id <USERNAME>@<MAC_HOST_IP>
```

Update your Ansible inventory to include the Mac host details wherein you replace **<MAC_HOST_IP>** and **<USERNAME>** with the appropriate values for your Mac host.

Test the Connection

Create a simple Ansible playbook to test the connection to the Mac host:

```
nano ~/GitforGits/playbooks/test_mac_connection.yml
```

Add the script as given below:

```
---

- name: Test Connection to Mac Host

  hosts: mac

  tasks:

    - name: Ping the Mac host

      ping:
```

Run the playbook using the **ansible-playbook** command:

```
ansible-playbook
~/GitforGits/playbooks/test_mac_connection.yml
```

If the setup is correct, you should see a successful response indicating that Ansible can communicate with the Mac host via SSH.

Install Homebrew on Mac Host

Homebrew is a popular package manager for macOS. It allows you to install software and manage dependencies easily. To install Homebrew, run the following command on the Mac host:

```
/bin/bash -c "$(curl -fsSL
https://raw.githubusercontent.com/Homebrew/install/HEAD/i
nstall.sh)"
```

Verify that Homebrew is installed correctly by running the following command on the Mac host:

```
brew --version
```

Manage Software on Mac

Create a new playbook to manage software on the Mac host using Homebrew:

```
nano ~/GitforGits/playbooks/manage_software_mac.yml
```

Add the script as given below:

```
---

- name: Manage Software on Mac

  hosts: mac

  tasks:

    - name: Ensure Homebrew is installed
```

```
      command: /bin/bash -c "$(curl -fsSL
https://raw.githubusercontent.com/Homebrew/install/HEAD/i
nstall.sh)"

      args:

        creates: /usr/local/bin/brew


    - name: Install Git using Homebrew

      homebrew:

        name: git

        state: present


    - name: Install wget using Homebrew

      homebrew:

        name: wget

        state: present
```

Execute as below:

```
ansible-playbook
~/GitforGits/playbooks/manage_software_mac.yml
```

Once you've followed these steps, Ansible can be used to manage Mac systems. Through this setup, you can effortlessly incorporate Mac hosts into your current automation workflows while taking advantage of Ansible's robust automation features for remote host management and configuration.

Recipe #7: Managing Mac Hosts

Once you have set up Ansible to manage Mac systems, you can perform various administrative tasks to ensure these systems are properly configured and maintained. This recipe will cover some common tasks, such as gathering system information, managing files, creating users, and configuring services on Mac hosts.

Gather System Information

Create a playbook to gather system information from the Mac host:

```
nano ~/GitforGits/playbooks/mac_system_info.yml
```

Add the following code snippet:

```
---

- name: Gather System Information

  hosts: mac

  tasks:

    - name: Gather facts about the Mac host

      setup:
```

Run the playbook to gather system information:

```
ansible-playbook
~/GitforGits/playbooks/mac_system_info.yml
```

This playbook uses the **setup** module to gather information about the Mac host, such as operating system version, hardware details, and more.

Manage Files on Mac

Create a playbook to manage files on the Mac host, such as creating, deleting, and copying files:

```
nano ~/GitforGits/playbooks/mac_manage_files.yml
```

Add the script as given below:

```yaml
---
- name: Manage Files on Mac
  hosts: mac
  tasks:
    - name: Create a directory
      file:
        path: /tmp/example
        state: directory

    - name: Create a file
      copy:
        content: "This is a test file."
        dest: /tmp/example/testfile.txt

    - name: Delete a file
      file:
        path: /tmp/example/testfile.txt
        state: absent
```

Run the playbook to manage files on the Mac host:

```
ansible-playbook
~/GitforGits/playbooks/mac_manage_files.yml
```

This playbook uses the **file** and **copy** modules to create a directory, create a file with specific content, and delete a file.

Create and Manage Users

Create a playbook to create and manage users on the Mac host:

```
nano ~/GitforGits/playbooks/mac_manage_users.yml
```

Add the following code snippet:

```
---
- name: Manage Users on Mac
  hosts: mac
  tasks:
    - name: Create a user
      user:
        name: exampleuser
        password: "{{ 'Password123' |
password_hash('sha512') }}"
        state: present

    - name: Ensure user is an admin
      command: dseditgroup -o edit -a exampleuser -t user
admin
```

Run the playbook to manage users on the Mac host:

```
ansible-playbook
~/GitforGits/playbooks/mac_manage_users.yml
```

This playbook uses the **user** module to create a user and ensures that the user is an admin by adding them to the admin group.

Manage Services on Mac

Create a playbook to manage services on the Mac host:

```
nano ~/GitforGits/playbooks/mac_manage_services.yml
```

Add the script as given below:

```
---

- name: Manage Services on Mac

  hosts: mac

  tasks:

    - name: Ensure SSH service is running

      service:

        name: com.openssh.sshd

        state: started

        enabled: yes


    - name: Restart the syslog service

      command: sudo launchctl kickstart -k
system/com.apple.syslogd
```

Run the playbook to manage services on the Mac host:

```
ansible-playbook
~/GitforGits/playbooks/mac_manage_services.yml
```

This playbook uses the **service** module to ensure that the SSH service is running and enabled, and the **command** module to restart the syslog service.

Install Software on Mac

Create a playbook to install software on the Mac host using Homebrew:

```
nano ~/GitforGits/playbooks/install_software_mac.yml
```

Add the script as given below:

```
---

- name: Install Software on Mac

  hosts: mac

  tasks:

    - name: Ensure Homebrew is installed

      command: /bin/bash -c "$(curl -fsSL
https://raw.githubusercontent.com/Homebrew/install/HEAD/i
nstall.sh)"

      args:

        creates: /usr/local/bin/brew


    - name: Install Git using Homebrew

      homebrew:

        name: git
```

```
        state: present


    - name: Install wget using Homebrew
      homebrew:
        name: wget
        state: present
```

Run the playbook to install software on the Mac host:

```
ansible-playbook
~/GitforGits/playbooks/install_software_mac.yml
```

By following these steps, you have successfully managed Mac hosts using Ansible and can perform various administrative tasks, including gathering system information, managing files, creating users, managing services, and installing software.

Recipe #8: Automating Software Installation on Mac

Automating software installation on Mac systems using Ansible can significantly streamline the process of setting up and maintaining multiple Mac hosts. By leveraging the Homebrew package manager, you can install, update, and manage software packages efficiently.

Our goal in this recipe is to automate the installation of software on Mac systems using Ansible and Homebrew, ensuring consistency and efficiency across your Mac infrastructure.

To begin with, make sure that Homebrew is installed on your Mac hosts. If not, then follow the Recipe#6 to get it installed on your Mac host.

Automate Software Installation

Create a new playbook to automate the installation of various software packages using Homebrew. Open your playbook file:

```
nano
~/GitforGits/playbooks/automate_software_installation_mac
.yml
```

Add the script as given below:

```
---

- name: Automate Software Installation on Mac

  hosts: mac

  tasks:

    - name: Ensure Homebrew is installed

      command: /bin/bash -c "$(curl -fsSL
https://raw.githubusercontent.com/Homebrew/install/HEAD/i
nstall.sh)"

      args:

        creates: /usr/local/bin/brew


    - name: Install Git

      homebrew:

        name: git

        state: present


    - name: Install wget

      homebrew:
```

```
        name: wget
        state: present

    - name: Install Node.js
      homebrew:
        name: node
        state: present

    - name: Install Python 3
      homebrew:
        name: python
        state: present

    - name: Install Docker
      homebrew_cask:
        name: docker
        state: present
```

This playbook ensures that Homebrew is installed on the Mac hosts and then uses Homebrew to install various software packages, including Git, wget, Node.js, Python 3, and Docker.

Verify Installation

After the playbook has run, verify that the software packages have been installed on the Mac hosts. You can do this by running commands to check the versions of the installed software:

```
git --version

wget --version

node --version

python3 --version

docker --version
```

Sample Program: Installing Additional Software

To install additional software packages, you can modify the playbook to include more tasks. For example, to install Visual Studio Code and Slack, update the playbook as follows:

```
nano
~/GitforGits/playbooks/automate_software_installation_mac
.yml
```

Add the following tasks:

```
---

- name: Automate Software Installation on Mac

  hosts: mac

  tasks:

    - name: Ensure Homebrew is installed

      command: /bin/bash -c "$(curl -fsSL
https://raw.githubusercontent.com/Homebrew/install/HEAD/i
nstall.sh)"

      args:

        creates: /usr/local/bin/brew
```

```
- name: Install Git
  homebrew:
    name: git
    state: present

- name: Install wget
  homebrew:
    name: wget
    state: present

- name: Install Node.js
  homebrew:
    name: node
    state: present

- name: Install Python 3
  homebrew:
    name: python
    state: present

- name: Install Docker
```

```
      homebrew_cask:
        name: docker
        state: present

    - name: Install Visual Studio Code
      homebrew_cask:
        name: visual-studio-code
        state: present

    - name: Install Slack
      homebrew_cask:
        name: slack
        state: present
```

Execute the updated playbook using the **ansible-playbook** command:

```
ansible-playbook
~/GitforGits/playbooks/automate_software_installation_mac
.yml
```

After running the updated playbook, verify that Visual Studio Code and Slack have been installed on the Mac hosts. With this, you have successfully automated the installation of software on Mac systems using Ansible and Homebrew.

Summary

The purpose of this chapter was to demonstrate how to expand Ansible's automation capabilities to manage both Windows and Mac systems. For Windows, the initial step is to configure the requisite components on the Windows machine and the Linux control node in order to set up Ansible. This necessitated the activation of WinRM on Windows hosts and the verification that Ansible could communicate securely with these hosts. Next, you learned the management of Windows hosts by executing tasks such as configuring Windows services, managing files, creating users, and gathering system information. The capacity to install software on Windows using Ansible and Chocolatey was further addressed, illustrating the effective automation of software installations.

After migrating to Mac OS X, you can manage Mac hosts with Ansible by enabling SSH access and configuring key-based authentication. Homebrew, a widely used package manager for macOS, was installed to simplify the process of managing software. Managing Mac hosts entailed the following tasks: the collection of system information, the management of files, the creation of users, and the configuration of services using Ansible playbooks. You also ensured consistency and efficiency throughout your Mac infrastructure by automating software installation on Mac systems using Homebrew.

You should now have a solid grasp of how to manage and automate tasks on Windows and Mac systems using Ansible. This involved setting up protocols for remote management, carrying out routine administrative duties, and making sure that software installations were efficient and consistent across all hosts.

Knowledge Exercise

Question 1: What is the primary protocol used by Ansible to manage Windows hosts?
A) SSH
B) RDP
C) WinRM
D) SMB

Answer:
C) WinRM

Ansible uses Windows Remote Management (WinRM) as the primary protocol to manage Windows hosts, enabling remote execution of commands and tasks.

Question 2: Which Ansible module is used to install software on Windows using the Chocolatey package manager?
A) win_apt
B) win_package
C) win_chocolatey
D) win_msi

Answer:
C) win_chocolatey

The **win_chocolatey** module is used to install software on Windows hosts using the Chocolatey package manager.

Question 3: What command is used to enable WinRM on a Windows host?
A) Enable-WinRM
B) winrm quickconfig
C) start winrm
D) set winrm

Answer:
B) winrm quickconfig

The **winrm quickconfig** command is used to enable and configure WinRM on a Windows host for remote management.

Question 4: Which configuration file is updated to include Mac hosts in Ansible inventory?
A) /etc/ansible/ansible.cfg
B) ~/GitforGits/playbooks/hosts.yml
C) /etc/ansible/hosts
D) ~/GitforGits/inventory/hosts

Answer:
D) ~/GitforGits/inventory/hosts

The **~/GitforGits/inventory/hosts** file is updated to include Mac hosts in the Ansible inventory.

Question 5: How do you ensure that Homebrew is installed on a Mac host using Ansible?
A) Use the **mac_package** module
B) Use the **homebrew_cask** module
C) Use the **command** module with the Homebrew installation script
D) Use the **mac_software** module

Answer:
C) Use the **command** module with the Homebrew installation script

To ensure Homebrew is installed on a Mac host using Ansible, you use the **command** module with the Homebrew installation script.

Question 6: Which Ansible module is used to manage users on Mac systems?
A) user
B) mac_user
C) win_user
D) homebrew_user

Answer:
A) user

The **user** module is used to manage users on Mac systems, just as it is used on Linux systems.

Question 7: What is the correct syntax to restart a service on a Mac host using Ansible?
A) Use the **win_service** module
B) Use the **mac_service** module
C) Use the **launchctl** command with the **command** module
D) Use the **systemd** module

Answer:
C) Use the **launchctl** command with the **command** module

To restart a service on a Mac host, you use the **launchctl** command with the **command** module.

Question 8: What must be enabled on a Mac host to allow Ansible to manage it via SSH?
A) Remote Desktop
B) File Sharing
C) Remote Login
D) AirDrop

Answer:
C) Remote Login

Remote Login must be enabled on a Mac host to allow Ansible to manage it via SSH.

Question 9: Which Ansible module is used to manage file permissions on Mac hosts?
A) win_file
B) mac_permissions
C) file
D) mac_file

Answer:

C) file

The **file** module is used to manage file permissions on Mac hosts, just as it is used on Linux systems.

Question 10: What is the purpose of setting the **ansible_ssh_private_key_file** parameter in the inventory for Mac hosts?
A) To specify the location of the private key for SSH access
B) To enable password authentication for SSH
C) To disable SSH key-based authentication
D) To set the default SSH user for Ansible

Answer:
A) To specify the location of the private key for SSH access

The **ansible_ssh_private_key_file** parameter specifies the location of the private key for SSH access to Mac hosts.

Question 11: What does the **win_ping** module in Ansible do?
A) Installs software on Windows hosts
B) Configures services on Windows hosts
C) Checks the connectivity and validates the WinRM setup on Windows hosts
D) Copies files to Windows hosts

Answer:
C) Checks the connectivity and validates the WinRM setup on Windows hosts

The **win_ping** module checks the connectivity and validates the WinRM setup on Windows hosts.

Question 12: Which Ansible module would you use to install applications that are managed by Homebrew Cask on a Mac?
A) homebrew
B) cask
C) homebrew_cask
D) mac_app

Answer:
C) homebrew_cask

The **homebrew_cask** module is used to install applications that are managed by Homebrew

Cask on a Mac.

Question 13: How do you ensure a service is enabled and started on a Mac host using Ansible?
A) Use the **win_service** module with the **state** parameter set to **started**
B) Use the **launchctl** command with the **command** module
C) Use the **systemd** module with the **enabled** parameter set to **yes**
D) Use the **homebrew_service** module

Answer:
B) Use the **launchctl** command with the **command** module

To ensure a service is enabled and started on a Mac host, you use the **launchctl** command with the **command** module.

Question 14: What is the purpose of the **ansible_winrm_server_cert_validation** parameter in the Ansible inventory for Windows hosts?
A) To specify the type of WinRM authentication to use
B) To ignore certificate validation errors when using WinRM
C) To enable encryption for WinRM communication
D) To specify the Windows user account for WinRM access

Answer:
B) To ignore certificate validation errors when using WinRM

The **ansible_winrm_server_cert_validation** parameter is used to ignore certificate validation errors when using WinRM.

Question 15: Which command is used to copy the SSH public key to a Mac host for key-based authentication?
A) **ssh-copy-key**
B) **scp**
C) **ssh-add**
D) **ssh-copy-id**

Answer:
D) **ssh-copy-id**

The **ssh-copy-id** command is used to copy the SSH public key to a Mac host for key-based authentication.

Question 16: What is the purpose of the **args** parameter with the **creates** option in the

command module when installing Homebrew?
A) To specify additional arguments for the command
B) To ensure the command runs even if Homebrew is already installed
C) To skip running the command if the specified file exists
D) To create a new directory before running the command

Answer:
C) To skip running the command if the specified file exists

The **args** parameter with the **creates** option in the **command** module ensures the command is skipped if the specified file exists, indicating Homebrew is already installed.

Question 17: Which module would you use to manage the installation of Node.js on a Mac using Ansible?
A) mac_package
B) homebrew
C) npm
D) homebrew_cask

Answer:
B) homebrew

The **homebrew** module is used to manage the installation of Node.js on a Mac using Ansible.

Question 18: How do you ensure that a specific version of a package is installed on a Windows host using the **win_chocolatey** module?
A) Specify the **version** parameter
B) Use the **state** parameter with the value **latest**
C) Use the **force** parameter
D) Specify the **name** parameter with the version number

Answer:
A) Specify the **version** parameter

To ensure that a specific version of a package is installed on a Windows host using the **win_chocolatey** module, you specify the **version** parameter.

Question 19: Which Ansible module is used to gather detailed system information from a Mac host?
A) mac_facts
B) gather_facts

C) system_info
D) setup

Answer:
D) setup

The **setup** module is used to gather detailed system information from a Mac host.

Question 20: What is the purpose of the **start_mode** parameter in the **win_service** module?
A) To specify the startup type for a Windows service
B) To start the service immediately
C) To enable or disable the service
D) To restart the service

Answer:
A) To specify the startup type for a Windows service

The **start_mode** parameter in the **win_service** module is used to specify the startup type for a Windows service (e.g., automatic, manual, disabled).

Chapter 7: Ansible with AWS, Azure and GCP

Introduction

Using Ansible, you learned how to automate software installations, configure remote management protocols, and perform administrative tasks in the previous chapter. You also learned how to manage Windows and Mac systems. This chapter concentrates on three major cloud providers: AWS, Azure, and Google Cloud Platform (GCP) in order to enhance your automation capabilities in cloud environments.

First, you'll learn how to set up Ansible to communicate with Amazon Web Services (AWS), and then you'll use that setup to manage your EC2 instances and other AWS resources through the use of modules. This will cover the practical aspects of getting your AWS environment up and running and automating common tasks. Next, you will hands-on the efficient management of Azure resources and the deployment of virtual machines using Ansible in conjunction with Azure. You will acquire a deeper understanding of the integration of Azure with Ansible in order to optimize your cloud operations.

The final section of the chapter concentrates on GCP. You will acquire the knowledge necessary to automate the management of a variety of GCP resources and integrate Ansible with GCP. The purpose of each recipe in this chapter is to equip you with practical knowledge and hands-on experience in the automation of cloud infrastructure using Ansible, thereby improving your capacity to manage multi-cloud environments in a seamless manner.

Recipe #1: Configuring Ansible for AWS

Setting up Ansible to manage AWS resources requires configuring the necessary authentication and preparing your environment. This recipe will demonstrate the steps to configure Ansible to interact with AWS, enabling you to automate tasks such as provisioning instances and managing AWS services.

In this recipe, you will learn to configure Ansible for AWS by setting up the necessary credentials and preparing the environment for automation tasks.

Install AWS CLI and Boto3

Ensure that the AWS Command Line Interface (CLI) and Boto3, the AWS SDK for Python, are installed on your control node. These tools are required for Ansible to interact with AWS.

```
sudo apt update

sudo apt install awscli -y

sudo pip install boto3
```

Configure AWS CLI

Configure the AWS CLI with your AWS credentials. Run the following command and follow the prompts to enter your AWS Access Key ID, Secret Access Key, and default region.

```
aws configure
```

Create or update your Ansible configuration file (**ansible.cfg**) to include the AWS credentials. Open your Ansible configuration file:

```
nano ~/GitforGits/ansible.cfg
```

Add the following script, replacing **<AWS_ACCESS_KEY_ID>**, **<AWS_SECRET_ACCESS_KEY>**, and **<AWS_REGION>** with your actual AWS credentials and region:

```
[defaults]

host_key_checking = False

inventory = ./inventory


[aws]

aws_access_key_id = <AWS_ACCESS_KEY_ID>

aws_secret_access_key = <AWS_SECRET_ACCESS_KEY>

region = <AWS_REGION>
```

Create Ansible Inventory File for AWS

Create an inventory file to specify the AWS hosts you will manage:

```
nano ~/GitforGits/inventory/aws_hosts
```

Add the given below script to define your AWS inventory:

```
[aws]
aws_instance_1 ansible_host=<INSTANCE_PUBLIC_IP>
aws_instance_2 ansible_host=<INSTANCE_PUBLIC_IP>
```

Replace **<INSTANCE_PUBLIC_IP>** with the actual public IP addresses of your AWS instances.

Install and Test the Ansible AWS Collection

Install the Ansible AWS Collection to access the AWS modules provided by Ansible:

```
ansible-galaxy collection install amazon.aws
```

Create a playbook to test the AWS configuration by listing EC2 instances. Open a new playbook file:

```
nano ~/GitforGits/playbooks/test_aws_configuration.yml
```

Add the script as given below:

```
---
- name: Test AWS Configuration
  hosts: localhost
  tasks:
    - name: List EC2 instances
      amazon.aws.ec2_instance_info:
        region: "{{ lookup('env', 'AWS_REGION') }}"
      register: ec2_info
    - name: Display EC2 instances
```

```
    debug:
      var: ec2_info
```

Execute the playbook. If everything is configured correctly, you should see a list of your EC2 instances displayed in the output.

Recipe #2: Provisioning EC2 Instances

In this recipe, you will learn how to provision EC2 instances on AWS using Ansible. This involves creating a playbook to launch new instances based on your requirements.

Create EC2 Provisioning Playbook

Create a new playbook file to provision EC2 instances. Open your playbook file:

```
nano ~/GitforGits/playbooks/provision_ec2.yml
```

Add the following script to define the tasks for provisioning EC2 instances:

```
---
- name: Provision EC2 Instances
  hosts: localhost
  tasks:
    - name: Launch EC2 instance
      amazon.aws.ec2_instance:
        name: "GitforGits-Instance"
        key_name: "your_key_name"
        instance_type: "t2.micro"
        image_id: "ami-0abcdef1234567890"  # Replace with
a valid AMI ID
```

```
      wait: yes
      region: "{{ lookup('env', 'AWS_REGION') }}"
      count: 1
      state: present
      tags:
        Name: "GitforGits-Instance"
    register: ec2

  - name: Add new instance to inventory
    add_host:
      hostname: "{{ item.public_ip }}"
      groupname: aws
    loop: "{{ ec2.instances }}"

  - name: Wait for SSH to come up
    wait_for:
      host: "{{ item.public_ip }}"
      port: 22
      delay: 60
      timeout: 320
      state: started
```

```
    loop: "{{ ec2.instances }}"

  - name: Display instance details
    debug:
      var: ec2
```

This playbook will launch a new EC2 instance, add it to the Ansible inventory, and wait for SSH to be available.

Verify EC2 Instance

After the playbook has run, you can verify the EC2 instance in your AWS Management Console under the EC2 dashboard. Ensure that the instance has been launched with the specified configurations.

Recipe #3: Managing AWS Resources with Ansible Modules

In this recipe, you will learn how to manage various AWS resources using Ansible modules. This includes tasks such as creating S3 buckets, managing IAM roles, and working with other AWS services.

Create S3 Bucket

Create a new playbook to manage an S3 bucket. Open your playbook file:

```
nano ~/GitforGits/playbooks/manage_s3.yml
```

Add the given below script to create an S3 bucket:

```
---
- name: Manage S3 Bucket
  hosts: localhost
```

```
  tasks:
    - name: Create S3 bucket
      amazon.aws.s3_bucket:
        name: "gitforgits-bucket"
        state: present
        region: "{{ lookup('env', 'AWS_REGION') }}"
```

Create IAM Role

Create a new playbook to manage IAM roles. Open your playbook file:

```
nano ~/GitforGits/playbooks/manage_iam_role.yml
```

Add the given below script to create an IAM role:

```
---
- name: Manage IAM Role
  hosts: localhost
  tasks:
    - name: Create IAM role
      amazon.aws.iam_role:
        name: "GitforGitsRole"
        assume_role_policy_document: |
          {
            "Version": "2012-10-17",
            "Statement": [
```

```
            {
              "Effect": "Allow",
              "Principal": {
                "Service": "ec2.amazonaws.com"
              },
              "Action": "sts:AssumeRole"
            }
          ]
        }
      state: present
```

Create RDS Instance

Create a new playbook to manage RDS instances. Open your playbook file:

```
nano ~/GitforGits/playbooks/manage_rds.yml
```

Add the given below script to create an RDS instance:

```
---
- name: Manage RDS Instance
  hosts: localhost
  tasks:
    - name: Create RDS instance
      amazon.aws.rds_instance:
        db_instance_identifier: "gitforgits-db"
```

```
        db_instance_class: "db.t2.micro"
        engine: "mysql"
        master_username: "admin"
        master_user_password: "Password123"
        allocated_storage: 20
        state: present
        region: "{{ lookup('env', 'AWS_REGION') }}"
```

Execute the playbooks using the **ansible-playbook** command:

```
ansible-playbook ~/GitforGits/playbooks/manage_s3.yml
ansible-playbook
~/GitforGits/playbooks/manage_iam_role.yml
ansible-playbook ~/GitforGits/playbooks/manage_rds.yml
```

Verify AWS Resources

After running the playbooks, verify that the AWS resources have been created and configured correctly in the AWS Management Console. To do this, check the S3 buckets, IAM roles, and RDS instances to ensure they match the specified configurations. This approach allows you to automate the management of various AWS services to make the cloud infrastructure consistent and efficiently maintained.

Recipe #4: Using Ansible with Azure

Using Ansible with Azure is comparable to using Ansible with AWS in many ways. Both platforms leverage Ansible to automate cloud resource management, including provisioning virtual machines, configuring networks, and managing storage. Just as with AWS, you need to configure your environment with the necessary authentication details to allow Ansible to interact with Azure services. The Ansible modules for Azure provide similar functionalities to those for AWS, enabling you to manage various Azure resources seamlessly.

This recipe guides you to configure Ansible to work with Azure by setting up the necessary credentials and preparing the environment for automation tasks.

Install and Configure Azure CLI

Ensure that the Azure Command Line Interface (CLI) is installed on your control node:

```
curl -sL https://aka.ms/InstallAzureCLIDeb | sudo bash
```

Install the Ansible Azure Collection to access the Azure modules provided by Ansible:

```
ansible-galaxy collection install azure.azcollection
```

Authenticate the Azure CLI with your Azure account:

```
az login
```

Follow the prompts accordingly to authenticate with your Azure credentials.

Create Azure Service Principal

Create a Service Principal for Ansible to use for managing resources on Azure:

```
az ad sp create-for-rbac --name AnsibleServicePrincipal -
-role Contributor --scopes
/subscriptions/YOUR_SUBSCRIPTION_ID
```

Replace **YOUR_SUBSCRIPTION_ID** with your actual Azure subscription ID. Note the output values for **appId**, **password**, **tenant**, and **subscriptionId**.

Use the Azure Service Principal

To do this, create or update your Ansible configuration file (**ansible.cfg**) to include the Azure credentials. Open your Ansible configuration file:

```
nano ~/GitforGits/ansible.cfg
```

Add the given below script, replacing the placeholders with your actual Azure credentials:

```
[azure]
client_id = <APP_ID>
secret = <PASSWORD>
tenant = <TENANT_ID>
subscription_id = <SUBSCRIPTION_ID>
```

Create Ansible Inventory File for Azure

Create an inventory file to specify the Azure hosts you will manage:

```
nano ~/GitforGits/inventory/azure_hosts
```

Add the following code snippet:

```
[azure]
azure_host ansible_host=<VM_PUBLIC_IP>
```

Replace **<VM_PUBLIC_IP>** with the actual public IP address of your Azure virtual machine.

Test Azure Configuration

Create a playbook to test the Azure configuration by listing virtual machines. Open a new playbook file:

```
nano ~/GitforGits/playbooks/test_azure_configuration.yml
```

Add the script as given below:

```
---
- name: Test Azure Configuration
  hosts: localhost
```

```
tasks:

  - name: List Azure virtual machines

    azure.azcollection.azure_rm_virtualmachine_info:

      resource_group: myResourceGroup

    register: vm_info


  - name: Display virtual machines

    debug:

      var: vm_info
```

Now, after executing you should see a list of your Azure virtual machines displayed in the output. This setup enables you to automate various tasks in your Azure environment, such as provisioning virtual machines and managing other Azure resources.

Recipe #5: Deploying Virtual Machines on Azure

Deploying virtual machines (VMs) on Azure using Ansible allows you to automate the creation and management of VMs, ensuring consistency and efficiency in your cloud infrastructure. This recipe will instruct you step-by-step in creating and running a playbook to deploy VMs on Azure.

Create Resource Group

Create a playbook to create a resource group where the VM will be deployed. Open your playbook file:

```
nano ~/GitforGits/playbooks/create_resource_group.yml
```

Add the following code snippet:

```
---
```

```
- name: Create Azure Resource Group

  hosts: localhost

  tasks:

    - name: Create resource group

      azure.azcollection.azure_rm_resourcegroup:

        name: myResourceGroup

        location: eastus
```

Run the playbook to create the resource group:

```
ansible-playbook
~/GitforGits/playbooks/create_resource_group.yml
```

Create Virtual Network and Subnet

Create a playbook to set up a virtual network and subnet. Open your playbook file:

```
nano ~/GitforGits/playbooks/create_vnet_subnet.yml
```

Add the script as given below:

```
---

- name: Create Azure Virtual Network and Subnet

  hosts: localhost

  tasks:

    - name: Create virtual network

      azure.azcollection.azure_rm_virtualnetwork:

        name: myVNet
```

```
        resource_group: myResourceGroup
        address_prefixes: "10.0.0.0/16"
        location: eastus

    - name: Create subnet
      azure.azcollection.azure_rm_subnet:
        name: mySubnet
        resource_group: myResourceGroup
        virtual_network: myVNet
        address_prefix: "10.0.1.0/24"
```

Run the playbook to create the virtual network and subnet:

```
ansible-playbook
~/GitforGits/playbooks/create_vnet_subnet.yml
```

Create Public IP Address

Create a playbook to create a public IP address for the VM. Open your playbook file:

```
nano ~/GitforGits/playbooks/create_public_ip.yml
```

Add the following code snippet:

```
---
- name: Create Azure Public IP Address
  hosts: localhost
  tasks:
```

```
    - name: Create public IP
      azure.azcollection.azure_rm_publicipaddress:
        name: myPublicIP
        resource_group: myResourceGroup
        allocation_method: Dynamic
        location: eastus
```

Run the playbook to create the public IP address:

```
ansible-playbook
~/GitforGits/playbooks/create_public_ip.yml
```

Create Network Interface

Create a playbook to create a network interface for the VM. Open your playbook file:

```
nano ~/GitforGits/playbooks/create_network_interface.yml
```

Add the script as given below:

```
---
- name: Create Azure Network Interface
  hosts: localhost
  tasks:
    - name: Create network interface
      azure.azcollection.azure_rm_networkinterface:
        name: myNIC
        resource_group: myResourceGroup
```

```
        location: eastus
        virtual_network: myVNet
        subnet: mySubnet
        public_ip_name: myPublicIP
```

Run the playbook to create the network interface:

```
ansible-playbook
~/GitforGits/playbooks/create_network_interface.yml
```

Deploy Virtual Machine

Create a playbook to deploy the virtual machine. Open your playbook file:

```
nano ~/GitforGits/playbooks/deploy_vm.yml
```

Add the script as given below:

```
---
- name: Deploy Azure Virtual Machine
  hosts: localhost
  tasks:
    - name: Create virtual machine
      azure.azcollection.azure_rm_virtualmachine:
        resource_group: myResourceGroup
        name: myVM
        vm_size: Standard_B1s
        admin_username: azureuser
```

```
        admin_password: "Password123!"
        image:
          offer: UbuntuServer
          publisher: Canonical
          sku: 18.04-LTS
          version: latest
        network_interfaces: myNIC
```

Run the playbook to deploy the virtual machine:

```
ansible-playbook ~/GitforGits/playbooks/deploy_vm.yml
```

After the playbook has run, verify that the VM has been created in your Azure portal under the resource group **myResourceGroup**. This approach allows you to automate the deployment of VMs.

Recipe #6: Managing Azure Resources with Ansible

Managing Azure resources using Ansible allows you to automate tasks such as configuring virtual networks, managing storage accounts, and handling resource groups. This recipe will instruct you step-by-step in creating and running playbooks to manage various Azure resources.

Create Virtual Network and Subnet

Assuming you have already set up a resource group as shown in Recipe #5, create a new playbook to manage a virtual network and subnet. Open your playbook file:

```
nano ~/GitforGits/playbooks/manage_vnet_subnet.yml
```

Add the script as given below:

```
---
- name: Manage Azure Virtual Network and Subnet
  hosts: localhost
  tasks:
    - name: Ensure virtual network is present
      azure.azcollection.azure_rm_virtualnetwork:
        name: myManagedVNet
        resource_group: myResourceGroup
        address_prefixes: "10.1.0.0/16"
        location: eastus

    - name: Ensure subnet is present
      azure.azcollection.azure_rm_subnet:
        name: myManagedSubnet
        resource_group: myResourceGroup
        virtual_network: myManagedVNet
        address_prefix: "10.1.1.0/24"
```

Create Storage Account

Create a new playbook to manage a storage account. Open your playbook file:

```
nano ~/GitforGits/playbooks/manage_storage_account.yml
```

Add the following code snippet:

```
---
- name: Manage Azure Storage Account
  hosts: localhost
  tasks:
    - name: Ensure storage account is present
      azure.azcollection.azure_rm_storageaccount:
        name: myManagedStorageAccount
        resource_group: myResourceGroup
        location: eastus
        account_type: Standard_LRS
```

Create Azure SQL Database

Create a new playbook to manage an Azure SQL Database. Open your playbook file:

```
nano ~/GitforGits/playbooks/manage_sql_database.yml
```

Add the following code snippet:

```
---
- name: Manage Azure SQL Database
  hosts: localhost
  tasks:
    - name: Ensure SQL server is present
      azure.azcollection.azure_rm_sqlserver:
        resource_group: myResourceGroup
```

```
        name: myManagedSqlServer
        admin_username: sqladmin
        admin_password: "Password123!"
        location: eastus

    - name: Ensure SQL database is present
      azure.azcollection.azure_rm_sqldatabase:
        resource_group: myResourceGroup
        server_name: myManagedSqlServer
        name: myManagedDatabase
        edition: Basic
```

Run the Playbooks

Execute the playbooks using the **ansible-playbook** command:

```
ansible-playbook
~/GitforGits/playbooks/manage_vnet_subnet.yml

ansible-playbook
~/GitforGits/playbooks/manage_storage_account.yml

ansible-playbook
~/GitforGits/playbooks/manage_sql_database.yml
```

After running the playbooks, verify that the Azure resources have been created and configured correctly in the Azure portal. Check the virtual networks, storage accounts, and SQL databases to ensure they match the specified configurations.

Recipe #7: Integrating Ansible with Google Cloud

While AWS and Azure are popular cloud service providers with a wide range of services, Google Cloud Platform (GCP) offers unique advantages that can make it an attractive choice for many organizations. GCP is known for its high-performance computing, big data, and machine learning capabilities. It provides innovative services such as BigQuery for data warehousing and AI tools like TensorFlow. GCP also offers competitive pricing, strong support for open-source technologies, and robust global infrastructure. Integrating Ansible with GCP allows you to leverage these benefits while automating your cloud infrastructure.

With this recipe, you will understand to configure Ansible to work with GCP by setting up the necessary credentials and preparing the environment for automation tasks.

Install Google Cloud SDK

Ensure that the Google Cloud SDK is installed on your control node:

```
curl -sSL https://sdk.cloud.google.com | bash

exec -l $SHELL

gcloud init
```

Now, follow the prompts to authenticate with your Google Cloud account and set up your default project.

Install Ansible GCP Collection

Install the Ansible GCP Collection to access the GCP modules provided by Ansible:

```
ansible-galaxy collection install google.cloud
```

Create a service account for Ansible to use for managing resources on GCP. In the GCP Console, go to the IAM & Admin section, then Service Accounts, and create a new service account. Grant it the necessary permissions (e.g., Compute Admin, Storage Admin).

Download the JSON key file for the service account and store it on your control node.

Use the Service Account

Set the environment variable to use the service account key file. Open your **.bashrc** or

.bash_profile file and add the following line:

```
export GCP_SERVICE_ACCOUNT_FILE=/path/to/your/service-account-key.json
```

Source the file to apply the changes:

```
source ~/.bashrc  # or source ~/.bash_profile
```

Ansible Inventory File for GCP

Create an inventory file to specify the GCP hosts you will manage:

```
nano ~/GitforGits/inventory/gcp_hosts
```

Add the script as given below:

```
[gcp]

gcp_instance_1 ansible_host=<INSTANCE_PUBLIC_IP>

gcp_instance_2 ansible_host=<INSTANCE_PUBLIC_IP>
```

Replace **<INSTANCE_PUBLIC_IP>** with the actual public IP addresses of your GCP instances.

Test GCP Configuration

Create a playbook to test the GCP configuration by listing compute instances. Open a new playbook file:

```
nano ~/GitforGits/playbooks/test_gcp_configuration.yml
```

Put the following snippet:

```
---

- name: Test GCP Configuration
```

```
  hosts: localhost
  tasks:
    - name: List GCP compute instances
      google.cloud.gcp_compute_instance_info:
        auth_kind: serviceaccount
        service_account_file: "{{ lookup('env',
'GCP_SERVICE_ACCOUNT_FILE') }}"
        project: "your-gcp-project-id"
        zone: "us-central1-a"
      register: gcp_info

    - name: Display compute instances
      debug:
        var: gcp_info
```

You should see a list of your GCP compute instances displayed in the output. This setup enables you to automate various tasks in your GCP environment, such as provisioning instances and managing other GCP resources.

Recipe #8: Automating GCP Resource Management

Automating GCP resource management using Ansible allows you to handle tasks such as provisioning virtual machines, managing storage, and configuring networks efficiently. This recipe will instruct you step-by-step in creating and running playbooks to manage various GCP resources. This is donr by creating and running playbooks that utilize GCP-specific Ansible modules.

Provision a Virtual Machine

To begin with, create a playbook to provision a virtual machine on GCP. Open your playbook file:

```
nano ~/GitforGits/playbooks/provision_gcp_vm.yml
```

Put the following snippet:

```
---
- name: Provision GCP Virtual Machine
  hosts: localhost
  tasks:
    - name: Create a GCP VM instance
      google.cloud.gcp_compute_instance:
        name: "gitforgits-vm"
        machine_type: "n1-standard-1"
        zone: "us-central1-a"
        project: "your-gcp-project-id"
        auth_kind: serviceaccount
        service_account_file: "{{ lookup('env',
'GCP_SERVICE_ACCOUNT_FILE') }}"
        disk:
          - auto_delete: true
            boot: true
            source:
```

```
          image: "debian-9"
      network_interfaces:
        - network: "default"
          access_configs:
            - name: "External NAT"
              type: "ONE_TO_ONE_NAT"
```

Create Storage Bucket

Create a playbook to manage a storage bucket on GCP. Open your playbook file:

```
nano ~/GitforGits/playbooks/manage_gcp_storage.yml
```

Put the following snippet:

```
---
- name: Manage GCP Storage Bucket
  hosts: localhost
  tasks:
    - name: Create a GCP storage bucket
      google.cloud.gcp_storage_bucket:
        name: "gitforgits-bucket"
        location: "US"
        project: "your-gcp-project-id"
        auth_kind: serviceaccount
```

```
        service_account_file: "{{ lookup('env',
'GCP_SERVICE_ACCOUNT_FILE') }}"
```

Create a Virtual Network

Create a playbook to manage a virtual network on GCP. Open your playbook file:

```
nano ~/GitforGits/playbooks/manage_gcp_vnet.yml
```

Put the following snippet:

```
---
- name: Manage GCP Virtual Network
  hosts: localhost
  tasks:
    - name: Create a GCP virtual network
      google.cloud.gcp_compute_network:
        name: "gitforgits-vnet"
        project: "your-gcp-project-id"
        auth_kind: serviceaccount
        service_account_file: "{{ lookup('env',
'GCP_SERVICE_ACCOUNT_FILE') }}"
        auto_create_subnetworks: yes
```

Execute the playbooks using the **ansible-playbook** command:

```
ansible-playbook
~/GitforGits/playbooks/provision_gcp_vm.yml
```

```
ansible-playbook
~/GitforGits/playbooks/manage_gcp_storage.yml

ansible-playbook
~/GitforGits/playbooks/manage_gcp_vnet.yml
```

After running the playbooks, verify that the GCP resources have been created and configured correctly in the GCP Console. Check the compute instances, storage buckets, and virtual networks to ensure they match the specified configurations.

Summary

One of the things that you learned in this chapter was how to extend the automation capabilities of Ansible to include AWS, Azure, and GCP. To begin with, you configured Ansible to interact with AWS by establishing the requisite credentials and preparing the environment. You subsequently developed playbooks to provision EC2 instances and manage AWS resources, including S3 buckets, IAM roles, and RDS instances, thereby illustrating the seamless integration of Ansible with AWS.

Next, you studied the integration of Ansible with Azure, which involved the configuration of the environment to utilize Azure credentials and the development of playbooks to manage Azure resources. You acquired the skills necessary to establish resource groups, virtual networks, subnets, public IP addresses, and network interfaces, and subsequently deployed virtual machines on Azure.

Lastly, the chapter addressed the integration of Ansible with GCP by installing the Google Cloud SDK and establishing a service account for authentication. You developed playbooks to manage GCP resources, which encompassed the provisioning of virtual machines, the management of storage buckets, and the configuration of virtual networks. These example jobs showed how Ansible can automate a number of GCP management tasks.

In summary, you have gained the knowledge necessary to set up Ansible with any cloud provider, make and execute resource provisioning and management playbooks, and guarantee reliable and consistent cloud operations.

Knowledge Exercise

Question 1: Which command is used to install the AWS CLI on a Linux control node?
A) **sudo apt install awscli**
B) **sudo yum install awscli**

C) **curl -sL https://awscli.amazonaws.com | bash**
D) All of the above

Answer:
D) All of the above

The AWS CLI can be installed on a Linux control node using package managers like **apt** or **yum**, or directly from the official AWS CLI installation script.

Question 2: What is the purpose of the **boto3** library in the context of Ansible and AWS?
A) To manage Azure resources
B) To provide the AWS SDK for Python
C) To install Ansible on the control node
D) To configure GCP authentication

Answer:
B) To provide the AWS SDK for Python

The **boto3** library is the AWS SDK for Python and is required for Ansible to interact with AWS services.

Question 3: Which Ansible module is used to create an EC2 instance on AWS?
A) **ec2_instance**
B) **aws_instance**
C) **amazon.aws.ec2_instance**
D) **aws.ec2_instance**

Answer:
C) **amazon.aws.ec2_instance**

The **amazon.aws.ec2_instance** module is used to create and manage EC2 instances on AWS.

Question 4: Which command is used to authenticate the Azure CLI with your Azure account?
A) **az configure**
B) **az login**
C) **az auth**
D) **az setup**

Answer:
B) **az login**

The **az login** command is used to authenticate the Azure CLI with your Azure account.

Question 5: In the context of Ansible and Azure, what is the purpose of creating a Service Principal?
A) To manage GCP resources
B) To install the Azure CLI
C) To provide a security identity for automated access to Azure resources
D) To create virtual networks

Answer:
C) To provide a security identity for automated access to Azure resources

A Service Principal provides a security identity that Ansible can use to automate access to Azure resources.

Question 6: Which module is used to manage Azure virtual machines with Ansible?
A) **azure_rm_vm**
B) **azure_vm**
C) **azure.azcollection.azure_rm_virtualmachine**
D) **az.vm**

Answer:
C) **azure.azcollection.azure_rm_virtualmachine**

The **azure.azcollection.azure_rm_virtualmachine** module is used to manage Azure virtual machines with Ansible.

Question 7: Which Google Cloud service account file environment variable must be set for Ansible to authenticate with GCP?
A) **GCP_CREDENTIALS_FILE**
B) **GCP_KEY_FILE**
C) **GCP_SERVICE_ACCOUNT_FILE**
D) **GCP_AUTH_FILE**

Answer:
C) **GCP_SERVICE_ACCOUNT_FILE**

The **GCP_SERVICE_ACCOUNT_FILE** environment variable must be set to the path of the service account key file for Ansible to authenticate with GCP.

Question 8: Which module is used to create a virtual machine on GCP with Ansible?

A) **gcp_compute_instance**
B) **google.cloud.gcp_compute_instance**
C) **gcp_vm**
D) **google_compute_instance**

Answer:
B) **google.cloud.gcp_compute_instance**

The **google.cloud.gcp_compute_instance** module is used to create and manage virtual machines on GCP with Ansible.

Question 9: What is the primary advantage of using the **google.cloud** Ansible collection for GCP resource management?
A) It allows Ansible to manage AWS resources.
B) It provides modules specifically designed for interacting with GCP services.
C) It installs the Google Cloud SDK automatically.
D) It configures Azure services.

Answer:
B) It provides modules specifically designed for interacting with GCP services.

The **google.cloud** Ansible collection provides modules specifically designed for managing GCP resources, enabling efficient automation.

Question 10: Which Ansible module is used to manage storage buckets on GCP?
A) **gcp_storage**
B) **google_cloud_storage**
C) **google.cloud.gcp_storage_bucket**
D) **gcp_bucket**

Answer:
C) **google.cloud.gcp_storage_bucket**

The **google.cloud.gcp_storage_bucket** module is used to manage storage buckets on GCP with Ansible.

Question 11: What is the main purpose of setting up an inventory file for cloud hosts in Ansible?
A) To install the cloud provider's SDK
B) To configure authentication credentials
C) To define the hosts and groups that Ansible will manage

D) To create virtual machines

Answer:
C) To define the hosts and groups that Ansible will manage

An inventory file defines the hosts and groups that Ansible will manage, specifying their connection details.

Question 12: Which module is used to manage IAM roles on AWS with Ansible?
A) **aws_iam_role**
B) **amazon.aws.iam_role**
C) **aws_role**
D) **iam_role**

Answer:
B) **amazon.aws.iam_role**

The **amazon.aws.iam_role** module is used to manage IAM roles on AWS with Ansible.

Question 13: Which Azure module would you use to create a storage account with Ansible?
A) **azure_storage**
B) **azure.azcollection.azure_rm_storageaccount**
C) **az_storage**
D) **azure_storageaccount**

Answer:
B) **azure.azcollection.azure_rm_storageaccount**

The **azure.azcollection.azure_rm_storageaccount** module is used to create and manage storage accounts on Azure with Ansible.

Question 14: What does the **google.cloud.gcp_compute_network** module do?
A) It creates and manages virtual networks on GCP.
B) It provisions EC2 instances on AWS.
C) It configures virtual machines on Azure.
D) It manages IAM roles on GCP.

Answer:
A) It creates and manages virtual networks on GCP.

The **google.cloud.gcp_compute_network** module is used to create and manage virtual networks on GCP.

Question 15: Which command initializes the Google Cloud SDK on a control node?
A) **gcloud init**
B) **gcp init**
C) **google init**
D) **cloud init**

Answer:
A) **gcloud init**

The **gcloud init** command initializes the Google Cloud SDK on a control node.

Question 16: In the context of Ansible and cloud platforms, what is the role of a service account?
A) To manage DNS settings
B) To provide a security identity for automated resource management
C) To install Ansible on remote hosts
D) To configure network interfaces

Answer:
B) To provide a security identity for automated resource management

A service account provides a security identity that Ansible can use for automated resource management on cloud platforms.

Question 17: Which module would you use to create a resource group in Azure with Ansible?
A) **az_resource_group**
B) **azure.azcollection.azure_rm_resourcegroup**
C) **resource_group**
D) **azure_group**

Answer:
B) **azure.azcollection.azure_rm_resourcegroup**

The **azure.azcollection.azure_rm_resourcegroup** module is used to create and manage resource groups in Azure with Ansible.

Question 18: What is the purpose of the **azure.azcollection.azure_rm_virtualnetwork** module in Ansible?
A) To create virtual machines on Azure

B) To manage storage accounts on Azure
C) To create and manage virtual networks on Azure
D) To handle IAM roles on Azure

Answer:
C) To create and manage virtual networks on Azure

The **azure.azcollection.azure_rm_virtualnetwork** module is used to create and manage virtual networks on Azure.

Question 19: Which environment variable should be set to use a GCP service account key file with Ansible?
A) **GOOGLE_APPLICATION_CREDENTIALS**
B) **GCP_AUTH_FILE**
C) **GCP_KEY_PATH**
D) **GOOGLE_CLOUD_KEYFILE_JSON**

Answer:
A) **GOOGLE_APPLICATION_CREDENTIALS**

The **GOOGLE_APPLICATION_CREDENTIALS** environment variable should be set to the path of the GCP service account key file for Ansible to use it.

Question 20: Which Ansible module is used to gather information about EC2 instances on AWS?
A) **aws_instance_info**
B) **ec2_info**
C) **amazon.aws.ec2_instance_info**
D) **aws.ec2_info**

Answer:
C) **amazon.aws.ec2_instance_info**

The **amazon.aws.ec2_instance_info** module is used to gather information about EC2 instances on AWS.

CHAPTER 8: MANAGING CI/CD

Introduction

Building and automating build, test, and deployment procedures is a breeze with Ansible for CI/CD pipelines, which will be covered in this chapter. Initially, you will configure Ansible to operate within CI/CD environments, thereby ensuring complete automation and seamless integration. Following this, you will integrate Ansible with Jenkins, a widely used automation server, to efficiently manage the build and deployment processes. This encompasses the automation of duties such as code compilation, testing, and deployment to various environments.

Additionally, you will gain knowledge on how to automate your workflows using GitLab's integrated CI/CD capabilities and Ansible. The implementation of continuous delivery with Ansible will demonstrate how to verify that your code modifications are automatically deployed to production environments in a secure and dependable manner. Finally, learning how to manage rollbacks and version control with Ansible will enable you to maintain robust version control practices and gracefully address deployment failures.

Upon completion of this chapter, you will be well versed with methods by which Ansible can be employed to automate and improve your CI/CD processes, which improves the efficiency, reliability, and scalability of your software development and deployment workflows.

Recipe #1: Setting up Ansible for CI/CD Pipelines

This recipe will instruct you step-by-step in configuring Ansible to be used within CI/CD environments, ensuring it is ready to automate various tasks as part of your pipelines. The learnings behind this recipe is to configure Ansible to integrate seamlessly with CI/CD pipelines, enabling automated build, test, and deployment processes.

To begin with, ensure Ansible is installed on your control node. If it is not installed, refer to previous chapter for installation instructions.

Ansible Configuration for CI/CD

Update your Ansible configuration to optimize it for use in CI/CD environments. Open your Ansible configuration file:

```
nano ~/GitforGits/ansible.cfg
```

Add or update the given below script:

```
[defaults]
```

```
inventory = ./inventory

retry_files_enabled = False

log_path = ./ansible.log


[ssh_connection]

ssh_args = -o ControlMaster=auto -o ControlPersist=60s
```

This configuration sets the inventory file location, disables retry files, and enables logging. It also optimizes SSH connections for faster task execution.

Create Ansible Inventory File

Define the hosts and groups that Ansible will manage in the inventory file, so this file can be used by your CI/CD pipelines to target specific environments:

```
 [webservers]

webserver1 ansible_host=192.168.1.10 ansible_user=ubuntu


[databases]

dbserver1 ansible_host=192.168.1.20 ansible_user=ubuntu
```

Replace the IP addresses and usernames with your actual server details.

Environment Variables for CI/CD

Ensure that your CI/CD pipeline has access to necessary environment variables. For example, if you are using Jenkins, you can set these variables in the Jenkins job configuration. Common variables include:

- **ANSIBLE_HOST_KEY_CHECKING=False**
- **ANSIBLE_FORCE_COLOR=True**

These variables disable host key checking and force colored output, respectively.

Create Basic Playbook for Testing

Create a simple Ansible playbook to verify the setup. Open a new playbook file:

```
nano ~/GitforGits/playbooks/test_playbook.yml
```

Add the following code snippet:

```
---

- name: Test Playbook

  hosts: all

  tasks:

    - name: Ping all hosts

      ping:
```

This playbook uses the **ping** module to check connectivity with all hosts defined in the inventory. In your CI/CD tool (e.g., Jenkins, GitLab CI), configure a job to run the Ansible playbook. For example, in Jenkins, create a new job and add a build step to execute the Ansible playbook:

```
ansible-playbook ~/GitforGits/playbooks/test_playbook.yml
```

By following these steps, you have set up Ansible for CI/CD pipelinesand ensured that Ansible can be used effectively to automate tasks within CI/CD workflows.

Recipe #2: Integrating Ansible with Jenkins

Integrating Ansible with Jenkins allows automating the execution of Ansible playbooks as part of your CI/CD pipeline, which ultimately allows Jenkins to handle complex deployment processes efficiently using Ansible's powerful automation capabilities. In this recipe, you will learn to configure Jenkins to run Ansible playbooks as part of your build and deployment processes.

Install Ansible Plugin for Jenkins

To enable Jenkins to run Ansible playbooks, install the Ansible plugin. Navigate to Jenkins Dashboard and go to **Manage Jenkins** > **Manage Plugins**. Under the **Available** tab, search for

"Ansible" and install the Ansible plugin. If the plugin is already installed, you can skip this step.

After installing the plugin, configure it to specify the path to the Ansible executable. Go to **Manage Jenkins** > **Global Tool Configuration**, scroll down to the **Ansible** section, and click on **Add Ansible**. Fill in the **Name** field (e.g., **Ansible**) and specify the path to the Ansible executable (usually **/usr/bin/ansible** or **/usr/local/bin/ansible**).

Create a Jenkins Job

Create a new Jenkins job to run an Ansible playbook. From the Jenkins Dashboard, click on **New Item**, enter a name for the job (e.g., **Run Ansible Playbook**), select **Freestyle project**, and click **OK**.

In the job configuration page, set up your source control repository. Under the **Source Code Management** section, select your repository type (e.g., **Git**) and provide the repository URL and credentials if necessary.

Add a Build Step to Run Playbook

In the **Build** section of the job configuration, click on **Add build step** and select **Invoke Ansible Playbook**. Configure the build step with the following details:

- **`Playbook Path`**: The path to your Ansible playbook (e.g., **`~/GitforGits/playbooks/deploy_app.yml`**).
- **`Inventory`**: The path to your inventory file (e.g., **`~/GitforGits/inventory/hosts`**).

You can also specify additional options such as extra variables, tags, and limit. Once done, save the job configuration and trigger the job manually to ensure everything is set up correctly. Then, go to the job page and click on **Build Now**. Monitor the build progress and check the console output for any errors.

After the job completes, verify that the Ansible playbook executed successfully by checking the console output in Jenkins. With these steps, you have successfully integrated Ansible with Jenkins to automate the execution of Ansible playbooks.

Recipe #3: Automating Build and Deployment Processes

In this recipe, we will automate the build and deployment process for the GitforGits web application, which has been referenced in previous chapters.

To begin with, first ensure that the GitforGits application repository is set up correctly and accessible via your version control system. The repository should include all necessary files for building and deploying the application. From the Jenkins Dashboard, click on **New Item**, enter a name for the job (e.g., **GitforGits CI/CD Pipeline**), select **Pipeline**, and click **OK**.

Configure Pipeline Script

In the job configuration page, scroll down to the **Pipeline** section. Select **Pipeline script** from the **Definition** dropdown. Enter the following pipeline script:

```
pipeline {
    agent any
    environment {
        ANSIBLE_CONFIG = "${WORKSPACE}/ansible.cfg"
    }
    stages {
        stage('Checkout') {
            steps {
                git branch: 'main', url:
'https://github.com/yourusername/GitforGits.git'
            }
        }
        stage('Build') {
            steps {
                sh 'echo "Building the application..."'
                // Add build steps here, e.g., compiling
code, running tests, etc.
            }
```

```
        }
        stage('Deploy') {
            steps {
                ansiblePlaybook(
                    playbook:
'playbooks/deploy_gitforgits.yml',
                    inventory: 'inventory/hosts'
                )
            }
        }
    }
    post {
        success {
            echo 'Deployment successful!'
        }
        failure {
            echo 'Deployment failed!'
        }
    }
}
```

Replace **https://github.com/yourusername/GitforGits.git** with the actual URL of your GitforGits repository.

Ansible Playbook for Deployment

Create a playbook for deploying the GitforGits application. Open your playbook file:

```
nano ~/GitforGits/playbooks/deploy_gitforgits.yml
```

Put the following snippet:

```
---
- name: Deploy GitforGits Application
  hosts: webservers
  tasks:
    - name: Pull latest code from repository
      git:
        repo:
'https://github.com/yourusername/GitforGits.git'
        dest: /var/www/gitforgits
        version: main

    - name: Install dependencies
      command: npm install
      args:
        chdir: /var/www/gitforgits

    - name: Build the application
```

```
    command: npm run build
    args:
      chdir: /var/www/gitforgits

  - name: Restart web server
    service:
      name: nginx
      state: restarted
```

Configure Ansible Inventory

Ensure your Ansible inventory includes the details of the web servers where the application will be deployed:

```
[webservers]
webserver1 ansible_host=192.168.1.10 ansible_user=ubuntu
```

Replace the IP address and username with your actual server details. Then, save the Jenkins pipeline job configuration and manually trigger the job by clicking on **Build Now** on the job page. Monitor the build and deployment process through the Jenkins console output.

After the pipeline completes, verify that the GitforGits application has been deployed successfully. Check the application on the web server to ensure it is running as expected.

Recipe #4: Using Ansible with GitLab CI/CD

Integrating Ansible with GitLab CI/CD allows you to automate the build, test, and deployment processes of your applications directly within GitLab. This recipe will instruct you to integrate Ansible with GitLab CI/CD and automate the deployment of the GitforGits web application.

Create GitLab CI/CD Configuration File

Create a **.gitlab-ci.yml** file in the root of your GitforGits repository to define your CI/CD pipeline. This file will contain the instructions for GitLab to build, test, and deploy your application using Ansible.

```
stages:
  - build
  - deploy
variables:
  ANSIBLE_CONFIG: "${CI_PROJECT_DIR}/ansible.cfg"

build:
  stage: build
  script:
    - echo "Building the application..."
    # Add build steps here, e.g., compiling code, running
tests, etc.

deploy:
  stage: deploy
  before_script:
    - apt-get update
    - apt-get install -y ansible
  script:
    - ansible-playbook -i inventory/hosts
playbooks/deploy_gitforgits.yml
```

```
  environment:
    name: production
  only:
    - main
```

This configuration defines two stages: **build** and **deploy**. The **build** stage runs any necessary build steps, while the **deploy** stage installs Ansible and runs the Ansible playbook for deployment. The playbook should be located in the **playbooks** directory and be named **deploy_gitforgits.yml**. If not already created, refer to Recipe #3 for creating this playbook.

Push Changes to GitLab

Commit and push the **.gitlab-ci.yml** file and any other changes to your GitforGits repository on GitLab.

```
git add .gitlab-ci.yml
git commit -m "Add GitLab CI/CD configuration"
git push origin main
```

Once you push the changes, GitLab will automatically trigger the pipeline. Go to your GitLab project and navigate to **CI / CD** > **Pipelines** to monitor the pipeline execution. Check the logs to ensure that the build and deploy stages complete successfully.

With these steps, you have now successfully integrated Ansible with GitLab CI/CD to automate the build and deployment process of the GitforGits web application.

Recipe #5: Implementing Continuous Delivery with Ansible

Continuous Delivery (CD) ensures that code changes are automatically prepared for a release to production. By integrating Ansible with your CI/CD pipelines, you can automate the deployment process and ensure that your applications are always in a deployable state. In this recipe, you will learn to set up a Continuous Delivery pipeline, ensuring that code changes are automatically deployed to a staging or production environment.

Define the Continuous Delivery Pipeline in GitLab

First, ensure that your GitLab CI/CD pipeline is set up to automate the build, test, and deployment processes. The **.gitlab-ci.yml** file should be configured to include stages for continuous delivery. Then, create or open the **.gitlab-ci.yml** file in the root of your GitforGits repository and add the given below script:

```
stages:

  - build

  - test

  - deploy


variables:

  ANSIBLE_CONFIG: "${CI_PROJECT_DIR}/ansible.cfg"


build:

  stage: build

  script:

    - echo "Building the application..."

    # Add build steps here, e.g., compiling code, running
tests, etc.


test:

  stage: test

  script:
```

```
    - echo "Running tests..."
    # Add test steps here, e.g., unit tests, integration tests, etc.

deploy_staging:
  stage: deploy
  script:
    - apt-get update
    - apt-get install -y ansible
    - ansible-playbook -i inventory/hosts playbooks/deploy_gitforgits.yml
  environment:
    name: staging
    url: http://staging.gitforgits.com
  only:
    - develop

deploy_production:
  stage: deploy
  script:
    - apt-get update
    - apt-get install -y ansible
```

```
    - ansible-playbook -i inventory/hosts
playbooks/deploy_gitforgits.yml
  environment:
    name: production
    url: http://production.gitforgits.com
  only:
    - main
```

This configuration includes stages for building, testing, and deploying the application. The **deploy_staging** job deploys the application to a staging environment when changes are pushed to the **develop** branch, while the **deploy_production** job deploys to production when changes are pushed to the **main** branch.

Create Playbooks for Staging and Production

Here, you need to have separate Ansible playbooks for deploying to staging and production environments. For this, we will assume a single playbook that handles both environments based on variables. To begin with, open your playbook file:

```
nano ~/GitforGits/playbooks/deploy_gitforgits.yml
```

Add or update the given below script to handle different environments:

```
---
- name: Deploy GitforGits Application
  hosts: webservers
  vars:
    environment: "{{ env }}"
  tasks:
    - name: Pull latest code from repository
```

```
    git:
      repo:
'https://github.com/yourusername/GitforGits.git'
      dest: /var/www/gitforgits
      version: main

  - name: Install dependencies
    command: npm install
    args:
      chdir: /var/www/gitforgits

  - name: Build the application
    command: npm run build
    args:
      chdir: /var/www/gitforgits

  - name: Restart web server
    service:
      name: nginx
      state: restarted
```

Update the inventory file:

```
[staging]

staging_webserver ansible_host=192.168.1.30
ansible_user=ubuntu

[production]

production_webserver ansible_host=192.168.1.40
ansible_user=ubuntu
```

Replace the IP addresses and usernames with your actual server details.

Push Changes to GitLab

Commit and push the **.gitlab-ci.yml** file and any other changes to your GitforGits repository on GitLab.

```
git add .gitlab-ci.yml

git commit -m "Add GitLab CI/CD configuration for
Continuous Delivery"

git push origin develop
```

Verify the Pipeline Execution

Once you push the changes, GitLab will automatically trigger the pipeline. Go to your GitLab project and navigate to **CI / CD** > **Pipelines** to monitor the pipeline execution. Check the logs to ensure that the build, test, and deploy stages complete successfully.

After the pipeline completes, verify that the GitforGits application has been deployed successfully to the staging environment. Merge the changes from **develop** to **main** to trigger the deployment to the production environment and verify the deployment there as well.

Recipe #6: Managing Rollbacks and Version Control

To keep your application deployments, stable and reliable, you must manage rollbacks and version control. To properly manage rollbacks, this recipe outlines steps to configure your CI/CD pipeline and our goal in this recipe is to manage rollbacks and version control so that you can revert to a previous stable version if a deployment fails.

Prepare Application Repository

Ensure that the GitforGits application repository is set up correctly on GitLab and includes version tags for releases and also very important is that each version tag should correspond to a stable release of the application.

Create a Rollback Playbook

Create a new Ansible playbook to handle rollbacks. This playbook will revert the application to a specified previous version. Open your playbook file:

```
nano ~/GitforGits/playbooks/rollback_gitforgits.yml
```

Put the following snippet:

```
---
- name: Rollback GitforGits Application
  hosts: webservers
  vars:
    version: "{{ version }}"
  tasks:
    - name: Pull specific version from repository
      git:
        repo:
'https://github.com/yourusername/GitforGits.git'
        dest: /var/www/gitforgits
        version: "{{ version }}"
```

```
    - name: Install dependencies
      command: npm install
      args:
        chdir: /var/www/gitforgits

    - name: Build the application
      command: npm run build
      args:
        chdir: /var/www/gitforgits

    - name: Restart web server
      service:
        name: nginx
        state: restarted
```

Configure GitLab CI/CD for Rollbacks

Update your **.gitlab-ci.yml** file to include a job for handling rollbacks. Open or create the **.gitlab-ci.yml** file in the root of your GitforGits repository and add the given below script:

```
stages:
  - build
  - test
  - deploy
```

```
  - rollback

variables:
  ANSIBLE_CONFIG: "${CI_PROJECT_DIR}/ansible.cfg"

build:
  stage: build
  script:
    - echo "Building the application..."
    # Add build steps here, e.g., compiling code, running
tests, etc.

test:
  stage: test
  script:
    - echo "Running tests..."
    # Add test steps here, e.g., unit tests, integration
tests, etc.

deploy:
  stage: deploy
  script:
```

```
    - apt-get update

    - apt-get install -y ansible

    - ansible-playbook -i inventory/hosts
playbooks/deploy_gitforgits.yml

  environment:

    name: production

    url: http://production.gitforgits.com

  only:

    - main


rollback:

  stage: rollback

  script:

    - apt-get update

    - apt-get install -y ansible

    - ansible-playbook -i inventory/hosts
playbooks/rollback_gitforgits.yml -e
"version=${ROLLBACK_VERSION}"

  environment:

    name: production

  when: manual
```

This configuration includes a **rollback** stage that runs the rollback playbook. The rollback job can be triggered manually and takes the **ROLLBACK_VERSION** variable to specify the version to revert to.

Then, commit and push the **.gitlab-ci.yml** file and any other changes to your GitforGits repository on GitLab.

```
git add .gitlab-ci.yml playbooks/rollback_gitforgits.yml

git commit -m "Add rollback configuration to GitLab CI/CD"

git push origin main
```

Trigger a Rollback

To trigger a rollback, go to your GitLab project and navigate to **CI / CD** > **Pipelines**. Find the latest pipeline run, and under the **rollback** stage, click on **Play**. Enter the version tag you want to roll back to in the **ROLLBACK_VERSION** variable prompt and confirm.

Keep an eye on the GitforGits program to make sure it has rolled back to the desired version after the rollback processes finish. Launch the web server program and verify it is running the expected version. This is how you use Ansible with GitLab CI/CD to create a rollback mechanism. If a deployment fails, you can easily restore to a stable version with this setup's version control and rollback management features.

Summary

This chapter taught you how to automate build, test, and deployment processes for the GitforGits web application by including Ansible with CI/CD pipelines. Starting Ansible for CI/CD pipelines, the chapter started with making sure it was set up right to operate in these contexts. Then you combined Ansible with Jenkins to let the Jenkins build and deployment procedures automatically run Ansible playbooks. Jenkins could effectively manage challenging deployment chores with this arrangement.

Then, concentrating on the GitforGits application, you automated the build and deployment procedures with Ansible and Jenkins. To guarantee a consistent and simplified deployment process, you built a Jenkins pipeline with phases for developing, testing, and application deployment. Additionally covered was the integration of Ansible with GitLab CI/CD, in which you set GitLab to automatically deploy the GitforGits application. This includes configuring a.gitlab-ci.yml file to specify the pipeline phases and including Ansible deployment using playbooks.

The chapter also looked at building continuous delivery so that code changes are automatically ready for deployment to production. In GitLab, you create a continuous delivery pipeline that lets you automatically deploy depending on branch changes into staging and production environments. The Ansible module for managing rollbacks and version control was finally covered. If a deployment fails, you may go back to a prior stable version by building a rollback plan and setting GitLab CI/CD to manage rollbacks.

By the end of this chapter, you knew exactly how to use Ansible to automate CI/CD tasks and integrate with GitLab and Jenkins to improve your deployment practices.

Knowledge Exercise

Question 1: What is the primary benefit of integrating Ansible with CI/CD pipelines?
A) Manual deployment of applications
B) Automated and consistent build, test, and deployment processes
C) Enhanced graphical user interface for Ansible
D) Increased need for manual intervention

Answer:
B) Automated and consistent build, test, and deployment processes

Integrating Ansible with CI/CD pipelines automates and ensures consistency in build, test, and deployment processes, reducing the need for manual intervention.

Question 2: Which Jenkins plugin is required to run Ansible playbooks within Jenkins jobs?
A) Docker Plugin
B) Git Plugin
C) Ansible Plugin
D) Pipeline Plugin

Answer:
C) Ansible Plugin

The Ansible Plugin is required to run Ansible playbooks within Jenkins jobs, enabling seamless integration.

Question 3: In a Jenkins pipeline, what is the purpose of the **ansiblePlaybook** step?
A) To define Git repositories
B) To compile code
C) To execute Ansible playbooks
D) To restart Jenkins

Answer:

C) To execute Ansible playbooks

The **ansiblePlaybook** step in a Jenkins pipeline is used to execute Ansible playbooks as part of the build or deployment process.

Question 4: Which file in the GitLab repository defines the CI/CD pipeline configuration?
A) **Jenkinsfile**
B) **docker-compose.yml**
C) **.gitlab-ci.yml**
D) **ansible.cfg**

Answer:
C) **.gitlab-ci.yml**

The **.gitlab-ci.yml** file in the GitLab repository defines the CI/CD pipeline configuration, specifying stages, jobs, and scripts to run.

Question 5: How can you trigger a rollback in GitLab CI/CD using Ansible?
A) By merging to the main branch
B) By running a manual job with the rollback stage
C) By pushing code changes
D) By creating a new repository

Answer:
B) By running a manual job with the rollback stage

In GitLab CI/CD, you can trigger a rollback by running a manual job that includes the rollback stage, specifying the version to revert to.

Question 6: Which Ansible module is used to pull code from a Git repository during deployment?
A) **file**
B) **copy**
C) **git**
D) **command**

Answer:
C) **git**

The **git** module is used in Ansible playbooks to pull code from a Git repository during the deployment process.

Question 7: What is the purpose of the **environment** section in a GitLab CI/CD job definition?
A) To install Ansible
B) To define the job's execution environment and URL
C) To run unit tests
D) To compile the application

Answer:
B) To define the job's execution environment and URL

The **environment** section in a GitLab CI/CD job definition specifies the job's execution environment and the URL of the deployed application.

Question 8: In continuous delivery, what triggers the deployment to the production environment in GitLab CI/CD?
A) Changes pushed to the **develop** branch
B) A manual trigger by the user
C) Changes pushed to the **main** branch
D) Running unit tests

Answer:
C) Changes pushed to the **main** branch

In continuous delivery with GitLab CI/CD, deployment to the production environment is typically triggered by changes pushed to the **main** branch.

Question 9: What variable can you use in GitLab CI/CD to specify a version for rollback?
A) **ROLLBACK_VERSION**
B) **DEPLOY_VERSION**
C) **ROLLBACK_TAG**
D) **VERSION_CONTROL**

Answer:
A) **ROLLBACK_VERSION**

The **ROLLBACK_VERSION** variable is used in GitLab CI/CD to specify a version for rollback during a manual job execution.

Question 10: How do you install Ansible on a GitLab CI/CD runner during the deploy stage?
A) By using the **ansiblePlaybook** command
B) By running **apt-get install ansible** in the script section

C) By creating a Docker container
D) By pushing a new commit

Answer:
B) By running **apt-get install ansible** in the script section

To install Ansible on a GitLab CI/CD runner during the deploy stage, you run **apt-get install ansible** in the script section of the job definition.

Question 11: Which section in the **.gitlab-ci.yml** file defines the stages of the pipeline?
A) **variables**
B) **jobs**
C) **stages**
D) **environment**

Answer:
C) **stages**

The **stages** section in the **.gitlab-ci.yml** file defines the various stages of the CI/CD pipeline.

Question 12: Why is the **ansible.cfg** file important in CI/CD pipelines involving Ansible?
A) It specifies the Ansible version to use
B) It defines the configuration and behavior of Ansible
C) It contains environment variables for the pipeline
D) It lists the Git repositories to be cloned

Answer:
B) It defines the configuration and behavior of Ansible

The **ansible.cfg** file is crucial as it defines the configuration and behavior of Ansible, ensuring consistency during pipeline executions.

Question 13: Which command is used to update package lists before installing Ansible in a CI/CD script?
A) **sudo apt update**
B) **yum update**
C) **dnf update**
D) **brew update**

Answer:
A) **sudo apt update**

The **sudo apt update** command is used to update package lists on Debian-based systems before installing Ansible in a CI/CD script.

Question 14: What is the purpose of the **manual** keyword in the GitLab CI/CD job definition?
A) To run the job automatically
B) To allow the job to be triggered manually
C) To schedule the job
D) To disable the job

Answer:
B) To allow the job to be triggered manually

The **manual** keyword allows a GitLab CI/CD job to be triggered manually rather than automatically as part of the pipeline.

Question 15: Which command would you use in a GitLab CI/CD job to pull a specific version of code from a Git repository?
A) **git commit**
B) **git fetch**
C) **git pull**
D) **git checkout <version>**

Answer:
D) **git checkout <version>**

The **git checkout <version>** command is used to pull a specific version of code from a Git repository in a GitLab CI/CD job.

Question 16: What stage is responsible for deploying the application in a CI/CD pipeline?
A) **build**
B) **test**
C) **deploy**
D) **rollback**

Answer:
C) **deploy**

The **deploy** stage is responsible for deploying the application in a CI/CD pipeline.

Question 17: In Jenkins, what is the purpose of the **post** block in a pipeline script?
A) To define environment variables

B) To specify actions to be taken after the pipeline stages complete
C) To compile the application
D) To install dependencies

Answer:
B) To specify actions to be taken after the pipeline stages complete

The **post** block in a Jenkins pipeline script specifies actions to be taken after the pipeline stages complete, such as sending notifications or archiving artifacts.

Question 18: What does the **environment** keyword do in the context of a GitLab CI/CD job?
A) Sets up the operating system for the job
B) Specifies the target deployment environment
C) Defines environment variables for the job
D) Configures the network settings

Answer:
B) Specifies the target deployment environment

The **environment** keyword in a GitLab CI/CD job specifies the target deployment environment, such as staging or production.

Question 19: Which Ansible module can be used to restart a web server as part of a deployment?
A) **copy**
B) **file**
C) **service**
D) **shell**

Answer:
C) **service**

The **service** module is used to manage services on a target system, including restarting a web server as part of a deployment.

Question 20: How do you ensure that the correct version of the application is deployed during a rollback?
A) By using the **git** module with the **version** parameter
B) By manually editing the source code
C) By running unit tests
D) By changing the branch in the repository

Answer:
A) By using the **git** module with the **version** parameter

To ensure that the correct version of the application is deployed during a rollback, you use the **git** module with the **version** parameter to pull the specific version from the repository.

CHAPTER 9: ANSIBLE TOWER AND AWX

Introduction

So far, you worked from Ansible's setup and writing playbooks to inventory management, using advanced playbook approaches, and connecting Ansible with cloud platforms including AWS, Azure, and GCP. Using Jenkins and GitLab, you explored CI/CD process automation; you also handled rollbacks and continuous delivery. This expertise prepares you to efficiently automate, simplify your IT processes.

In this final chapter, you will learn about Ansible Tower and AWX, two powerful tools that provide enterprise-level features for managing Ansible automation at scale. With Ansible Tower, a web-based solution, users have a centralized platform to manage workflows, inventory, and playbooks. A similar set of tools and functionalities are available in AWX, the open-source alternative to Ansible Tower.

First things first: get Ansible Tower up and running, then create up projects and manage inventory. You will then develop and oversee task templates, which specify Tower's execution of playbooks. After that, you will look at configuring and running AWX to offer a reasonably priced Ansible automation solution. You will also understand Tower API job and process scheduling, automation task automation, monitoring and reporting on automation activity. When you finish this chapter, you'll know how to use Ansible Tower and AWX to manage your Ansible automation in an effective and efficient way, taking your automation skills to the next level.

Recipe #1: Configuring Ansible Tower

It is absolutely necessary to configure Ansible Tower in order to manage your Ansible automation on a large scale. The objective of this recipe is to set up Ansible Tower so that your Ansible processes, inventory, and playbooks can be managed.

If Ansible Tower is not already installed, follow the below steps to install it. The installation process requires a running instance of PostgreSQL and other dependencies.

Install Ansible Tower

Download the Ansible Tower installation package from the Red Hat website. Once downloaded, extract the package.

```
tar -xvzf ansible-tower-setup-latest.tar.gz

cd ansible-tower-setup-*
```

Edit the **inventory** file to configure your PostgreSQL database, admin user credentials, and other necessary settings.

```
nano inventory
```

Add or update the given below script with your configuration details:

```
[tower]

localhost ansible_connection=local


[database]

host='localhost'

port='5432'

name='awx'

user='awx'

password='awxpassword'

admin_user='awx'

admin_password='awxpassword'
```

Execute the setup script to install Ansible Tower.

```
sudo ./setup.sh
```

Access Ansible Tower

Once the installation is complete, access Ansible Tower through your web browser. The default URL is **https://<tower_server_ip>**. Log in with the admin credentials you configured during the installation. After logging in, navigate to the **License** tab and upload your Ansible Tower license file. This license is required to activate all features of Ansible Tower.

Then, navigate to the **Settings** tab and configure the following basic settings:

- **Authentication:** Set up LDAP, SAML, or other authentication methods if required.
- **Notifications:** Configure email, Slack, or other notification integrations.

- **Jobs:** Set job settings such as timeouts, privileges, and output options.

Add Users, Teams and Organization

Go to the **Users** and **Teams** tabs to add users and create teams. Assign appropriate roles and permissions to each user and team to manage access to different resources and functionalities within Ansible Tower.

Navigate to the **Organizations** tab and create an organization. Ansible Tower's organizational units let you group related resources like inventory, projects, and job templates. Following these steps, Ansible Tower has been successfully configured. This configuration gives you a single location to manage all of your Ansible automation, which simplifies tasks like inventory management, workflow orchestration, and automation activity monitoring.

Recipe #2: Managing Projects and Inventories in Tower

Managing projects and inventories in Ansible Tower allows you to organize and control your Ansible playbooks and the systems they manage. In this recipe, you will learn how to manage the GitforGits project and the associated inventories in Ansible Tower.

This recipe guides you to create and manage projects and inventories in Ansible Tower for the GitforGits application.

Create Project in Ansible Tower

A project in Ansible Tower links to a source control repository containing your playbooks. To create a project for GitforGits:

1. Go to the Ansible Tower dashboard and click on `Projects` in the left-hand menu.
2. Click the **+** button to add a new project.
3. Fill in the necessary details:
    - **Name:** GitforGits Project
    - **Organization:** Select the organization you created in Recipe #1.
    - **SCM Type:** Git
    - **SCM URL:** `https://github.com/yourusername/GitforGits.git`
    - **SCM Branch/Tag/Commit:** Specify if needed (e.g., `main`).
    - **SCM Credential:** Select or create a credential if authentication is required.
4. Click `Save` to create the project. Ansible Tower will sync with the repository and pull the playbooks.

Create Inventory in Ansible Tower

Inventories in Ansible Tower are collections of hosts or groups of hosts you want to manage. To create an inventory for GitforGits:

1. Go to the Ansible Tower dashboard and click on **`Inventories`** in the left-hand menu.
2. Click the **+** button to add a new inventory.
3. Fill in the necessary details:
    - **Name:** GitforGits Inventory
    - **Organization:** Select the organization you created in Recipe #1.
4. Click **`Save`** to create the inventory.

Add Hosts to the Inventory

After creating the inventory, you need to add hosts that were defined in the previous chapters:

1. Within the GitforGits Inventory, go to the **`Hosts`** tab and click the **+** button to add new hosts.
2. Fill in the necessary details:
    - **Name:** webserver1
    - **Description:** Web Server for GitforGits
    - **Variables:** (Optional) Add any host-specific variables as needed.
3. Repeat this process for additional hosts, such as **`dbserver1`** if applicable.

Create Groups within Inventory

Groups allow you to categorize and organize hosts within an inventory. To create groups:

1. Within the GitforGits Inventory, go to the **`Groups`** tab and click the **+** button to add a new group.
2. Fill in the necessary details:
    - **Name:** Web Servers
    - **Description:** Group for all web servers.
3. After creating the group, navigate to the group's **`Hosts`** tab and add the relevant hosts (e.g., **`webserver1`**).
   Repeat this process for additional groups, such as a **`Database Servers`** group.

Verify the Project and Inventory Configuration

1. Navigate to the **`Projects`** page, select the GitforGits Project, and click the **`Sync`** button to ensure the latest playbooks are pulled from the repository.

2. To verify that the inventory is correctly configured, navigate to the **Inventories** page, select the GitforGits Inventory, and click on **Hosts**. Select a host and click **Run Command**. Execute a simple command, such as **ping**, to ensure Ansible Tower can communicate with the host.

After following these steps, you will have complete control over the GitforGits project and all of its related Ansible Tower inventories. The configuration provides a structured and efficient way to handle automation tasks by allowing you to organize and control your playbooks and the systems they manage.

Recipe #3: Creating and Managing Job Templates

Ansible Tower's job templates let you specify the playbook to run, the inventory to use, and any additional variables or settings for playbook execution. This recipe will teach you how to use Ansible Tower with the GitforGits app to make and manage job templates.

Create a Job Template

1. Go to the Ansible Tower dashboard and click on **Job Templates** in the left-hand menu.
2. Click the **+** button to add a new job template.
3. Fill in the necessary details:
    - **Name:** Deploy GitforGits
    - **Job Type:** Run
    - **Inventory:** Select the **GitforGits Inventory** you created in Recipe #2.
    - **Project:** Select the **GitforGits Project**.
    - **Playbook:** Select the playbook you want to run (e.g., **deploy_gitforgits.yml**).
    - **Credential:** Select or create a credential if authentication is required for the hosts.
4. Click **Save** to create the job template.

Schedule the Job

1. Go to the **Job Templates** page and find the **Deploy GitforGits** template you created.
2. Click the **Rocket** icon next to the job template to launch the job. This will run the specified playbook using the selected inventory and project.

3. Navigate to the **Jobs** page to monitor the progress of the job. Click on the job to view detailed output and ensure that all tasks are executed successfully.

To automate the execution of the job template, you can schedule it to run at specified intervals.

1. Go to the **Job Templates** page and select the **Deploy GitforGits** template.
2. Click on the **Schedule** tab and then click **+** to add a new schedule.
3. Fill in the necessary details:
    - **Name:** Daily Deployment
    - **Start Date:** Select the date and time to start the schedule.
    - **Repeat Frequency:** Set the frequency (e.g., daily, weekly).
4. Click **Save** to create the schedule.

To manage existing job templates, navigate to the **Job Templates** page. Here, you can edit, duplicate, or delete job templates as needed. Editing allows you to update the template configuration, such as changing the playbook or inventory. Duplicating a template creates a copy, which you can modify for different purposes without starting from scratch.

Use Job Templates in Workflows

Job templates can be combined into workflows to orchestrate complex automation processes. To create a workflow:

1. Go to the **Templates** page and click on the **+** button, then select **Workflow Template**.
2. Fill in the necessary details for the workflow template, such as **Name** and **Description**.
3. **Add Nodes:** In the workflow editor, add nodes representing job templates, project syncs, or inventory syncs. Connect the nodes to define the order and dependencies of the tasks.
4. Click **Save** to create the workflow template.

Workflows can be launched and monitored in the same way as job templates. Navigate to the **Templates** page, find the workflow template, and click the **Rocket** icon to launch it. Monitor the progress in the **Jobs** page to ensure all tasks are executed as expected. This setup allows you to define, schedule, and automate the execution of your playbooks, providing a structured and efficient way to handle your automation tasks.

Recipe #4: Setting up and using AWX

AWX is the open-source version of Ansible Tower, offering similar features and functionalities for managing Ansible automation. This recipe will instruct you step-by-step to set up AWX and use it to manage the GitforGits project and associated inventories.

Install Docker and Docker Compose

AWX runs as a set of Docker containers, so you need Docker and Docker Compose installed on your system. If not already installed, refer to official Docker documentation to install them on your system.

Clone the AWX Repository

Clone the official AWX repository from GitHub:

```
git clone https://github.com/ansible/awx.git

cd awx/installer
```

Edit the **inventory** file to configure AWX settings such as the admin user credentials and database settings:

```
nano inventory
```

Update the following settings as needed:

```
localhost ansible_connection=local
ansible_python_interpreter="/usr/bin/env python"


# Admin user settings

admin_user=admin

admin_password=admin_password


# PostgreSQL settings

postgres_data_dir="/var/lib/pgdocker"

pg_hostname="localhost"
```

```
pg_port="5432"

pg_database="awx"

pg_username="awx"

pg_password="awxpass"


# Other settings can be configured as needed
```

Deploy AWX

Execute the playbook to deploy AWX:

```
ansible-playbook -i inventory install.yml
```

This will pull the necessary Docker images, create the containers, and set up AWX.

Once the installation is complete, access AWX through your web browser. The default URL is **http://<your_server_ip>**. Log in with the admin credentials you configured in the inventory file.

Create a Project in AWX

To manage the GitforGits project in AWX, create a new project:

1. Go to the AWX dashboard and click on **`Projects`** in the left-hand menu.
2. Click the **+** button to add a new project.
3. Fill in the necessary details:
    - **Name:** GitforGits Project
    - **Organization:** Select the organization you created.
    - **SCM Type:** Git
    - **SCM URL:** **`https://github.com/yourusername/GitforGits.git`**
    - **SCM Branch/Tag/Commit:** Specify if needed (e.g., **`main`**).
    - **SCM Credential:** Select or create a credential if authentication is required.
4. Click **`Save`** to create the project. AWX will sync with the repository and pull the playbooks.

Inventory in AWX

To manage the inventories for GitforGits, create a new inventory:

1. Go to the AWX dashboard and click on **`Inventories`** in the left-hand menu.
2. Click the **+** button to add a new inventory.
3. Fill in the necessary details:
    - **Name:** GitforGits Inventory
    - **Organization:** Select the organization you created.
4. Click **`Save`** to create the inventory.

After creating the inventory, add hosts and groups:

1. Within the GitforGits Inventory, go to the **`Hosts`** tab and click the **+** button to add new hosts.
2. Fill in the necessary details:
    - **Name:** webserver1
    - **Description:** Web Server for GitforGits
    - **Variables:** (Optional) Add any host-specific variables as needed.
3. Repeat this process for additional hosts, such as **`dbserver1`** if applicable.
4. Navigate to the **`Groups`** tab and click the **+** button to add a new group. Add hosts to the groups as needed.

Create and Launch Job Templates

Create job templates to define how playbooks are executed:

1. Go to the **`Job Templates`** page and click the **+** button to add a new job template.
2. Fill in the necessary details:
    - **Name:** Deploy GitforGits
    - **Job Type:** Run
    - **Inventory:** Select the **`GitforGits Inventory`**.
    - **Project:** Select the **`GitforGits Project`**.
    - **Playbook:** Select the playbook to run (e.g., **`deploy_gitforgits.yml`**).
    - **Credential:** Select or create a credential if authentication is required.
3. Click **`Save`** to create the job template.
4. Navigate to the **`Job Templates`** page, find the **`Deploy GitforGits`** template, and click the **`Rocket`** icon to launch the job. Monitor the progress in the **`Jobs`** page to ensure successful execution.

Following these steps, you have effectively configured and utilized AWX to oversee the GitforGits project and inventory. In this setup, you can take advantage of AWX's robust features to efficiently manage, automate, and keep tabs on your Ansible automation jobs.

Recipe #5: Scheduling Jobs and Workflows in Tower

Scheduling jobs and workflows in Ansible Tower allows you to automate tasks at specific times or intervals, ensuring regular maintenance and deployments without manual intervention. This recipe will instruct you scheduling the jobs created in the previous recipes for the GitforGits project.

Our goal in this recipe is to schedule jobs and workflows in Ansible Tower for the GitforGits application, ensuring regular automated execution.

Navigate to Job Templates

1. Go to the Ansible Tower dashboard and click on **`Job Templates`** in the left-hand menu.
2. Find the **`Deploy GitforGits`** job template created in Recipe #3. Click on the name of the job template to open its details page.

Add a Schedule to the Job Template

1. On the job template details page, navigate to the **`Schedules`** tab. This tab shows all schedules associated with the job template.
2. Click the **+** button to add a new schedule. This will open the schedule configuration form.
3. Fill in the necessary details:
    - **Name:** Enter a descriptive name for the schedule (e.g., **`Daily Deployment`**).
    - **Description:** Provide a description of the schedule (e.g., **`Schedule to run the GitforGits deployment daily`**).
    - **Start Date/Time:** Select the date and time when you want the schedule to start. Click on the calendar icon to choose the date and time.
    - **Local Time Zone:** Ensure the time zone is set correctly according to your requirements.
4. Configure the repeat frequency for the schedule:
    - **Frequency:** Select **`Daily`** for a daily schedule.
    - **Interval:** Set the interval to **`1`** to run the job every day.
    - **End:** (Optional) Specify an end date for the schedule if it should stop at a certain point.

5. **Save the Schedule:** After configuring all the details, click **`Save`** to create the schedule. The new schedule will now appear under the **`Schedules`** tab for the job template.

Verify the Scheduled Job

1. Navigate to the **`Schedules`** tab on the job template's details page to see the newly created schedule. This tab lists all schedules associated with the job template, including their next run time.
2. Once the scheduled time is reached, the job will automatically run. To monitor its execution:
   - Go to the **`Jobs`** page from the Ansible Tower dashboard.
   - Look for the **`Deploy GitforGits`** job in the list of running or completed jobs.
   - Click on the job to view detailed output and ensure that all tasks were executed successfully.

Create a Workflow Job Template

If you have multiple job templates that need to be run in a specific sequence, you can create a workflow job template.

1. Go to the Ansible Tower dashboard and click on **`Templates`** in the left-hand menu, then select **`Workflow Job Templates`**.
2. Click the **+** button to add a new workflow job template.
3. Fill in the necessary details:
   - **Name:** Enter a name for the workflow (e.g., **`GitforGits Deployment Workflow`**).
   - **Description:** Provide a description for the workflow.
   - **Organization:** Select the organization created in Recipe #1.
4. In the workflow editor, click on the **+** button to add nodes. Each node represents a job template, project sync, or inventory sync. Connect the nodes to define the order and dependencies of the tasks.
   - For example, add the **`Deploy GitforGits`** job template as the first node.
5. Click **`Save`** to create the workflow job template.

Schedule the Workflow Job Template

1. Go to the **`Workflow Job Templates`** page and select the workflow template you just created.
2. Navigate to the **`Schedules`** tab and click the **+** button to add a new schedule.
3. Fill in the necessary details, similar to the steps outlined for scheduling a job template.

Ensure the start date, time, and repeat frequency are set according to your requirements. The, click **Save** to create the schedule for the workflow job template.

Verify the Scheduled Workflow

1. Navigate to the **Schedules** tab on the workflow job template's details page to see the newly created schedule.
2. Once the scheduled time is reached, the workflow will automatically run. To monitor its execution:
   - Go to the **Jobs** page from the Ansible Tower dashboard.
   - Look for the **GitforGits Deployment Workflow** in the list of running or completed jobs.
   - Click on the workflow to view detailed output and ensure that all tasks were executed successfully.

This configuration through the above steps ensures that your automation tasks run regularly and reliably, without the need for manual intervention.

Recipe #6: Using Tower API for Automation

Ansible Tower provides a RESTful API that allows you to automate tasks, integrate with other tools, and manage resources programmatically. This recipe will teach you to use the Ansible Tower API to automate job executions, retrieve job results, and manage resources.

Generate an API Token

To interact with the Tower API, you need to generate an API token.

1. Go to the Ansible Tower dashboard and click on your user profile in the top-right corner, then select **Tokens**.
2. Click the **+** button to generate a new token. Provide a description (e.g., **API Token for Automation**) and set the expiration date if needed.
3. Click **Save** to create the token. Copy the token value as you will need it for authentication in API requests.

Test API Authentication

Install an HTTP client like **curl** or a tool like **Postman** to send API requests. This recipe uses **curl** for demonstration.

Then, test the authentication by sending a request to the API as below:

```
curl -H "Authorization: Bearer <your_api_token>"
https://<tower_server_ip>/api/v2/me/
```

Replace **<your_api_token>** with the token you generated and **<tower_server_ip>** with the IP address of your Ansible Tower server. This request retrieves information about the authenticated user.

List Job Templates

To list job templates available in Ansible Tower, send the following request:

```
curl -H "Authorization: Bearer <your_api_token>"
https://<tower_server_ip>/api/v2/job_templates/
```

This request retrieves a list of all job templates.

Launch a Job Template

To launch a specific job template, you need its ID. Use the ID from the previous step to launch the job template.

```
curl -X POST -H "Authorization: Bearer <your_api_token>"
\

-H "Content-Type: application/json" \

-d '{"inventory": <inventory_id>}' \

https://<tower_server_ip>/api/v2/job_templates/<job_templ
ate_id>/launch/
```

Replace **<inventory_id>** with the ID of the inventory and **<job_template_id>** with the ID of the job template you want to launch. This request starts the specified job template.

Monitor Job Status

To monitor the status of a running job, use the job ID returned from the previous step.

```
curl -H "Authorization: Bearer <your_api_token>"
https://<tower_server_ip>/api/v2/jobs/<job_id>/
```

This request retrieves the status and details of the specified job. Also, to retrieve the results of a completed job, use the job ID as below:

```
curl -H "Authorization: Bearer <your_api_token>"
https://<tower_server_ip>/api/v2/jobs/<job_id>/stdout/
```

This request retrieves the standard output of the specified job, providing details about the execution.

Automate Job Executions

You can automate job executions by writing a script that uses the Tower API to trigger jobs based on certain conditions. Given below is an example using a Bash script:

```
#!/bin/bash

API_TOKEN="<your_api_token>"

TOWER_URL="https://<tower_server_ip>"

JOB_TEMPLATE_ID=<job_template_id>

INVENTORY_ID=<inventory_id>


# Launch Job Template

JOB_ID=$(curl -X POST -H "Authorization: Bearer
$API_TOKEN" \

-H "Content-Type: application/json" \

-d '{"inventory": '$INVENTORY_ID'}' \

$TOWER_URL/api/v2/job_templates/$JOB_TEMPLATE_ID/launch/
| jq -r '.id')
```

```
# Monitor Job Status

while true; do

  JOB_STATUS=$(curl -H "Authorization: Bearer $API_TOKEN"
$TOWER_URL/api/v2/jobs/$JOB_ID/ | jq -r '.status')

  if [[ "$JOB_STATUS" == "successful" ]]; then

    echo "Job $JOB_ID completed successfully."

    break

  elif [[ "$JOB_STATUS" == "failed" ]]; then

    echo "Job $JOB_ID failed."

    break

  else

    echo "Job $JOB_ID is $JOB_STATUS."

    sleep 10

  fi

done


# Retrieve Job Results

curl -H "Authorization: Bearer $API_TOKEN"
$TOWER_URL/api/v2/jobs/$JOB_ID/stdout/
```

This above script launches a job template, monitors its status, and retrieves the results upon completion.

You can also integrate the Tower API with other tools and platforms. For example, you can trigger

Ansible Tower jobs from a Jenkins pipeline or a GitLab CI/CD pipeline by using API calls within the pipeline scripts.

Summary

Ansible Tower and AWX, which you learned in this last chapter, offers a scalable and central platform for managing playbooks, inventories, and workflows; they also let you enhance your Ansible automation capabilities. The chapter started with configuring Ansible Tower, which involved setting up the platform, applying the relevant licenses, and creating organizations, users, and teams to control access and permissions. This setup made sure that automation operations could take place in a safe and organized setting.

You then looked into Ansible Tower's project and inventory management, with a focus on the GitforGits project. By establishing and setting projects and inventories, you may effectively arrange your playbooks and target hosts. This arrangement allowed you to define groups and hosts within inventories, which streamlined resource management. The chapter went on to explain how to create and manage job templates, which allow you to specify how playbooks are performed. You learnt how to set up job templates, schedule their execution, and track their progress. This method ensured that your automation duties were carried out regularly and reliably. You also built up and used AWX, the open-source version of Ansible Tower. This included installing AWX with Docker, configuring it, and managing projects and inventories in a manner similar to Ansible Tower. AWX offered a lower-cost option while maintaining similar functionality.

You also looked into scheduling jobs and workflows in Ansible Tower, which automates task execution at certain periods or intervals. This capability enables you to perform routine maintenance and deployments without requiring manual intervention. Finally, you used the Tower API for automation, learning how to generate API tokens, connect with the API via HTTP clients, and automate task executions programmatically. This integration enhances your automation skills by enabling smooth interaction with other tools and platforms.

Taken together, the skills you gained in this chapter will allow you to manage complicated workflows with ease and scale your automation efforts with precision, all thanks to Ansible Tower and AWX.

Knowledge Exercise

Question 1: What is the primary purpose of Ansible Tower and AWX?
A) To provide a centralized platform for managing playbooks, inventories, and workflows
B) To replace the need for Ansible playbooks
C) To create and manage Docker containers
D) To serve as a database management tool

Answer:
A) To provide a centralized platform for managing playbooks, inventories, and workflows

Ansible Tower and AWX are designed to offer a centralized and scalable platform for managing Ansible automation, including playbooks, inventories, and workflows.

Question 2: Which configuration file needs to be edited to set up AWX with Docker?
A) **ansible.cfg**
B) **inventory**
C) **.gitlab-ci.yml**
D) **Jenkinsfile**

Answer:
B) **inventory**

The **inventory** file is used to configure settings such as database credentials and admin user details when setting up AWX with Docker.

Question 3: How do you access Ansible Tower after installation?
A) By running a CLI command
B) Through a web browser at a specific URL
C) By logging into the server via SSH
D) By using a desktop application

Answer:
B) Through a web browser at a specific URL

After installation, Ansible Tower is accessed through a web browser using the URL of the Tower server.

Question 4: In Ansible Tower, what is the purpose of creating an organization?
A) To install Ansible on remote hosts
B) To group related resources and manage permissions
C) To automate the installation of Docker
D) To create virtual machines

Answer:
B) To group related resources and manage permissions

Creating an organization in Ansible Tower helps group related resources such as inventories, projects, and job templates, and manage user permissions.

Question 5: What is the role of a job template in Ansible Tower?
A) To store credentials for accessing remote hosts
B) To define how playbooks are executed, including inventory and extra variables
C) To manage Docker containers
D) To schedule database backups

Answer:
B) To define how playbooks are executed, including inventory and extra variables

A job template in Ansible Tower specifies the playbook to run, the inventory to use, and any extra variables or settings needed for execution.

Question 6: Which API request method is used to launch a job template in Ansible Tower?
A) GET
B) POST
C) PUT
D) DELETE

Answer:
B) POST

The **POST** method is used to launch a job template in Ansible Tower through the API.

Question 7: What is required to authenticate API requests to Ansible Tower?
A) SSH key
B) API token
C) User password
D) SSL certificate

Answer:
B) API token

An API token is required to authenticate API requests to Ansible Tower.

Question 8: How can you schedule a job template to run automatically at specific times in Ansible Tower?
A) By using the **cron** command
B) By creating a schedule in the **Schedules** tab of the job template
C) By configuring a Jenkins job
D) By setting up a GitLab pipeline

Answer:
B) By creating a schedule in the **Schedules** tab of the job template

In Ansible Tower, you can schedule a job template to run automatically by creating a schedule in the **Schedules** tab of the job template.

Question 9: What information is required when configuring a project in Ansible Tower?
A) Database credentials
B) SCM type and URL
C) Docker image name
D) Cloud provider credentials

Answer:
B) SCM type and URL

When configuring a project in Ansible Tower, you need to specify the SCM type (e.g., Git) and the repository URL.

Question 10: Which command is used to monitor the status of a running job in Ansible Tower via the API?
A) **curl -X GET**
B) **curl -X POST**
C) **curl -X PUT**
D) **curl -X DELETE**

Answer:
A) **curl -X GET**

The **GET** method is used to retrieve the status of a running job in Ansible Tower via the API.

Question 11: Which component in Ansible Tower allows you to group hosts logically?
A) Job templates
B) Projects
C) Inventories
D) Workflows

Answer:
C) Inventories

Inventories in Ansible Tower allow you to group hosts logically, organizing them for efficient management.

Question 12: What is the main advantage of using AWX over Ansible Tower?
A) Better performance
B) Cost-effectiveness as it is open-source
C) More features
D) Better user interface

Answer:
B) Cost-effectiveness as it is open-source

AWX is the open-source version of Ansible Tower, providing similar functionalities without the associated costs.

Question 13: In the context of Ansible Tower, what is a workflow?
A) A sequence of job templates and project syncs that run in a specific order
B) A method to create Docker containers
C) A type of inventory
D) A way to schedule jobs on remote hosts

Answer:
A) A sequence of job templates and project syncs that run in a specific order

A workflow in Ansible Tower is a sequence of job templates and project syncs that run in a specific order to automate complex processes.

Question 14: How can you add hosts to an inventory in Ansible Tower?
A) By importing a Docker image
B) By creating a schedule
C) By using the **Hosts** tab in the inventory
D) By configuring a Jenkins job

Answer:
C) By using the **Hosts** tab in the inventory

Hosts can be added to an inventory in Ansible Tower using the **Hosts** tab within the inventory configuration.

Question 15: What does the **Schedules** tab in a job template configuration allow you to do?
A) Define SCM types and URLs
B) Monitor running jobs
C) Set up automatic execution times for the job template
D) Manage API tokens

Answer:
C) Set up automatic execution times for the job template

The **Schedules** tab in a job template configuration allows you to set up automatic execution times for the job template.

Question 16: Which tool is used to install AWX?
A) Kubernetes
B) Docker and Docker Compose
C) Jenkins
D) GitLab CI

Answer:
B) Docker and Docker Compose

AWX is installed using Docker and Docker Compose.

Question 17: How can you trigger an Ansible Tower job from a Jenkins pipeline?
A) By using Jenkins's built-in scheduling
B) By configuring a Git hook
C) By making API calls to Ansible Tower from the Jenkins pipeline script
D) By using the **crontab** command

Answer:
C) By making API calls to Ansible Tower from the Jenkins pipeline script

You can trigger an Ansible Tower job from a Jenkins pipeline by making API calls to Ansible Tower from the pipeline script.

Question 18: What is the purpose of generating an API token in Ansible Tower?
A) To access the Tower user interface
B) To authenticate and authorize API requests
C) To create virtual machines
D) To manage Docker containers

Answer:
B) To authenticate and authorize API requests

Generating an API token in Ansible Tower is used to authenticate and authorize API requests.

Question 19: Which command retrieves the standard output of a completed job in Ansible

Tower via the API?
A) **curl -X GET /api/v2/jobs/<job_id>/**
B) **curl -X GET /api/v2/jobs/<job_id>/stdout/**
C) **curl -X POST /api/v2/jobs/<job_id>/**
D) **curl -X DELETE /api/v2/jobs/<job_id>/stdout/**

Answer:
B) **curl -X GET /api/v2/jobs/<job_id>/stdout/**

The command **curl -X GET /api/v2/jobs/<job_id>/stdout/** retrieves the standard output of a completed job in Ansible Tower via the API.

Question 20: What is the benefit of using job templates in Ansible Tower?
A) They create Docker containers automatically
B) They provide a way to define and standardize how playbooks are executed
C) They are used to install Ansible on remote hosts
D) They configure network settings

Answer:
B) They provide a way to define and standardize how playbooks are executed

Job templates in Ansible Tower provide a way to define and standardize how playbooks are executed, ensuring consistency and reliability in automation tasks.

Index

T

V

Y

Epilogue

It is my hope that, as we near the conclusion of the "Ansible DevOps Cookbook," you will take a moment to consider the path we have traveled and the wisdom we have gained. The idea for this book came from wanting to share useful solutions to problems that people face in the real world. It is now an entire book with over 75 and above recipes that will help you improve your DevOps skills when using Ansible. We've looked at the basics of setting up Ansible environments, writing good playbooks, and keeping track of inventories in these chapters. We've learned more advanced techniques, like how to automate cloud deployments and connect Ansible to CI/CD pipelines. Each recipe was made to solve a specific problem and includes clear, doable steps for setting it up and fixing any problems that come up.

Feedback and stories from readers like you have been some of the best parts of writing this book. It has been very satisfying to hear how these recipes have helped solve problems, streamline processes, and improve workflows in different businesses. That shows how powerful it is to work together and have the same goal: to make DevOps better and more efficient. These days, DevOps is changing quickly, and the tools and methods we use will also change along with it. Ansible will definitely stay an important part of automation strategies, and I hope this book will continue to help you as you face new challenges and take advantage of new opportunities. Along with the technical information you've learned, I hope this book has also given you the drive to keep getting better. Automation is not a one-time thing that needs to be done. If you adopt this way of thinking, you can keep improving and tweaking your workflows, which will keep your DevOps practices strong and flexible.

I think you should keep trying new things, learning, and telling other people about your experiences. Remember that you are part of a dynamic and helpful community as you work to solve a stubborn problem, improve a deployment process, or discover new ways to automate tasks. I appreciate that you picked this book to help you learn about Ansible and DevOps automation. Putting these recipes together has been an amazing journey, and I'm thrilled to share them with you. Your success is the best way to judge how useful this book is, and I can't wait to see how you use what you've learned in your work. Please accept my sincere appreciation for your willingness to read my experience around Ansible and DevOps. We look forward to many more successful deployments, streamlined processes, and new ideas.

Have fun automating!

Thorne Montgomery ☺

Thank You

www.ingramcontent.com/pod-product-compliance
Lightning Source LLC
Chambersburg PA
CBHW080209170726
48282CB00030B/1054
* 9 7 8 8 1 1 9 1 7 7 7 3 8 *